Image
Power

Top Image Experts Share
What to Know to Look Your Best

Power Dynamics Publishing
www.PowerDynamicsPub.com

PowerDynamics Publishing
www.powerdynamicspub.com

ISBN: 978-0-615-26175-1

Library of Congress Control Number: 2008909209

Printed in the United States of America

This book is printed on acid-free paper.

Acknowledgements

We dedicate this book to you, a woman who knows the power of presenting your best image. We know that you are ready to take steps to create positive change in your life—and we celebrate you!

Gratitude looks good on everyone. Before we share all our wisdom with you, we have a few people to thank for turning the idea of this book into a reality.

This book was the brilliant concept of Caterina Rando, a respected image business strategist, with whom many of us have worked to grow our businesses. She thought it would be valuable to hear from several top image experts on a variety of different image topics all at once—and we agreed. This book would not exist if not for her vision, her commitment to excellence, and her "take action" spirit. She was supported by a truly dedicated team who worked diligently to put together the best possible book. We are truly grateful for everyone's stellar contribution.

To Dortha Hise, who is always ready to take on any project and consistently provides great results with a smile, we wish we could all work with you all the time.

To Ruth Schwartz, whose many years of experience and wisdom served as an ongoing guide throughout the project. Your support is deeply appreciated.

To Susan Raab, who delivered some unique insight and clarification on the publishing process, we are truly grateful.

To Valerie Camarda whose excitement and expertise kept the project moving forward and graciously took on any challenges that arose, we very much appreciate your contribution.

To Barbara McDonald who brought her creative talent to the cover design, thank you for your patience with the many changes that were made to the many versions.

Of course we want to acknowledge each other for delivering outstanding information, guidelines and advice. Our dedication to uplifting the lives of women through image education goes far beyond the pages of this book. We consider ourselves truly blessed to do work that we love, and make a contribution to so many in the process. We do not take our good fortune lightly. We are clear on our mission here to make a genuine contribution to you—the reader. Thank you for granting us this extraordinary opportunity.

The Co-authors of Image Power

Table Of Contents

Introduction

Congratulations! You have opened a resource jam-packed with great ideas that will improve your life in ways you cannot yet imagine. You're about to discover the magic of *Image Power.*

Your personal image is so much more than hair, makeup and clothing. Your image is the message you send out to the world every time you walk in a room, meet someone new or talk on the phone. In fact, your image is the way you present yourself in *all* that you say and do! And of course, you want your image to be the best it can be.

With this book, you can quickly build your image power because as top experts in each of our respective specialties, we've banded together to give you the most powerful image strategies we know.

Each of us has seen how even small changes in your personal image can transform your self-confidence and uplift your life.

- A new custom-tailored suit boosts your self-assurance at work like nothing else.

- A new custom-fit bra that eliminates bulges and enhances your curves may add an attractive allure to your smile.

- Wearing colors that draw and hold the attention of others can help you make the right connections in your business and personal life.

- Knowing which fork to pick up first and mastering other etiquette details can lift you above your competition with poise, thoughtfulness and finesse.

With greater self confidence, you'll see your success soar—all because you took the time and effort to build your personal image and thereby your self confidence.

All the image professionals you will meet in this book want you to present yourself in a smart and savvy way. The key to this lies in finding the unique image that works best for *you*.

To get the most out of this book, read through it once cover to cover. Then go back and follow the tips that apply to you in the chapters most relevant to your current situation. With every image improvement you make, you'll see the world start responding to you in a new, more positive way.

Remember, just learning how to look your best will not transform your life. You must *take action* and apply the strategies, tips and tactics we share in these pages. Apply the many skills in this book and you will reap many rewards. With our knowledge and your action we are confident that like our thousands of satisfied clients, you too will master the magic of *Image Power*.
To your success!

The Co-authors of Image Power

Don't Get Down, Get Diva!

How Healthy Self-Care Positively Impacts Your Image—and Vice Versa

By Catherine Schuller, AICI CIP

We've all seen this Diva. She may not be the most gorgeous woman in the room, but she has a style that is purposeful and commanding. There is a certain glow about her. She is engaged and engaging, smiling, confident, and enjoying the moment. We all want to feel like that. It's contagious, electric and inspiring. It comes from being in control of yourself and your life. Being a Diva comes from taking care of yourself and loving yourself, and that looks good on everyone.

Viva La Diva

You picked up this book to enhance your image. The foundation for a great image on the outside is well-being and joy on the inside. Good health and happiness are alluring, energizing, and compelling. This comes from healthy self-care.

Taking care of our inner image is extra important for women. Researchers at the Society for the Advancement of Women's Health Research have concluded that women are two-to-three times more likely than men to suffer from depression because a woman's brain makes less of the hormone serotonin than a man's does. Also women comprise 80 percent of the population suffering from osteoporosis, which is attributable to a higher rate of lost bone mass. If you are wondering what any of this has to do with image, know that looking great and feeling great starts with what is going on inside you—not what you do on the outside.

I know this from my own personal experience. I found out how carrying 75 extra pounds for over ten years on my own frame had kicked in insulin resistance and pre-diabetes, and that if I was to stave off developing Type II diabetes I had to make major lifestyle changes in order to give myself an internal 'metabolic makeover.'

I never stopped caring about my appearance though. My hair, my makeup, and my wardrobe became more important than ever. As a result of my diagnosis I became distraught, and if it hadn't been for my belief in my worth and keeping up my image as a connection to my self-love, I may have given up. Maintaining my own positive Diva attitude has paid off, as I have learned how to take my personal quest and turn it into another new platform to reach the women I serve in the plus-size market. See the Resources at the end of this chapter for more information about *Divabetic*, an amazing program that helps women look great and get healthy.

Look vs. Outlook

Living life as a Diva can help you rise above the depression, obesity or whatever health challenge you might be facing. Ever notice that the first sign that a woman is getting better or on the mend (think of the hospital scene with Shirley MacLaine in Terms of Endearment), is that she wants to do her makeup and hair and spruce up a bit? In reality, who would think that insisting a patient do this would actually facilitate her road to recovery? There is an actual term for it, called "Appearance Related Side Effects" and it has been cited in studies and used in several innovative health programs dealing with stroke, cancer, and even domestic violence victims. It's almost as if attending to one's physical attributes triggers something in the deep recesses of the mind which sparks self-esteem. Attention to your image improves your self-image.

Discover Your Inner Diva

Whatever your challenge, the marrying of wellness and image is one which is crucial to your personal journey and can help you set your intention and find the fortitude to conquer the effects of disease, stay upbeat and on track about your care, maintaining a vibrant and healthy lifestyle to enable you to achieve your greater purpose. Yes, that's how important it is.

Image can provide the lifestyle transformation that has the ability to instill belief, motivation, and inspiration, as well as help in overcoming any insecurities that might hold us back. This is about using your inner Diva to support your health, whether it is for disease prevention, health maintenance or as an aid in staying on course after a diagnosis.

Carving out a healthy lifestyle is the key component to any successful image and cannot be overlooked. Taking into account the whole woman, head to toe, is truly an integrated modern approach that culminates in merging the disciplines of wardrobe and wellness. Whether women are confused about how to dress their curves or disheartened about a diagnosis, image is the ultimate connector and a powerful tool to banish depression and disbelief while delivering hope, courage and happiness.

We've heard the analogy, "Good paint on a bad canvas." This is about priming the canvas. All the makeup in the world can't improve what's not working underneath.

Achieving a Sense of Personal Worth

Our most difficult problem to overcome is often not pain but negativity. The antidote to a negative self-image is to have a strong sense of individual worth that does not depend on others or society for its existence. As a first step towards achieving a stronger sense of self-worth, ask yourself the following questions:

+ How do you feel about yourself right now?

+ How self-confident are you?

+ How would you like to feel about yourself?

So often we tend to give someone else the power to determine how we feel about ourselves, especially if we feel they disapprove of us because we have "let ourselves go" and become overweight or developed a medical condition. We must not give away our personal power to anyone. We must not let anyone else define who we are. We must, in a very positive way, determine who we are and stick to *our* definition.

+ Who or what makes you feel negative about yourself?

+ What are you going to do about it?

+ Do you have people in your life who think they have the right to offer opinions that might have a long-term negative impact on you?

+ Do you realize that achieving a sense of esteem—a strong sense of self—in the end is worth any amount of hard work?

Wellness and Image Go Hand in Hand

Knowing how to dress and use makeup can have a major impact on how you feel about yourself, and how well you take care of your health. This is true for all women (and men for that matter), not just women who are dealing with serious health issues such as cancer, obesity, diabetes, fibromyalgia or a myriad of other afflictions. Achieving self-confidence through a positive self-image and esteem are motivating byproducts to keeping on track, upbeat and inspired to do what you need to do to remain on your course of action.

Divas Take Action

Taking action is crucial to put a plan in gear that enables a Diva to successfully stay on-track and upbeat about her healthy self-care. There are many concrete steps you can take to make sure that you achieve consistency and commitment. When you notice things that continue to go undone, recognize that they are part of what you don't like, want to change and find motivation to improve. Making a list of goals to accomplish, and then choosing the most important ones is a great first step. There really is no better way than to create routines and practices that you incorporate into your daily existence. Check out the list below. Don't try these all at once, but look them over to see which ones immediately resonate. Pick your top five and go for it. Also, don't beat yourself up before you even start something new. Remember it takes 21-40 days to form a new habit. So go slow, and as Nike says "JUST DO IT." Before you know it, maybe as soon as a month, it will be incorporated into your daily routine and you will start to see the results.

Consistent Self Care Is Key

Before you start, please get a general health checkup, a mammogram, blood work, and a physical. Not doing so is like throwing darts at a dartboard in the dark. You may hit the mark, but you'll just be guessing. Either way, if you are dealing with a chronic health condition, a new diagnosis or just want to maintain optimum health, take a look at these ideas and find your top five to implement today!

- **Develop a daily Diva routine** to meet your image and health goals. Use image to trigger the overall practice of working toward wellness. Have a skincare, hair care, and body care regimen that keeps you going and glowing. Pampering is key to establishing deservingness and "Diva-tude."

- **Clean out closets and donate** the clothing you no longer want to charity. You can refer to Leah Oman's chapter in this book, "Get Out Of Your Closet in Seven Minutes—Looking Great!" to find out how to do this quickly and efficiently. Love what you have; have what you love.

- **Make a list of the pieces you need** to update your wardrobe—ones that will have you experience true joy when you wear them. Remember that inspiration and the wow factor are what you need to feed your new self-worth goal.

- **Have a shopping strategy for food** items that are nutrient dense and part of your meal plan goals. Strive to become a better eater, not a perfect eater.

- **Plan to work out**, and buy some outfits that will flatter you during your time at the gym. Don't just throw on faded and baggy sweats. A few coordinated pieces and a great pair of sneakers will make you feel polished and pulled together even on the stationary bike or elliptical machine. Exercise regularly—150 minutes a week. Thirty minutes a day can improve your diabetes numbers by 58 percent.

- **Start a walking program** with a buddy, if you don't want to attend a gym. Stick to it and make each other accountable. Get outside together and talk about your strides—literally. Walk the walk and talk the talk.

- **Make time to sleep at least eight hours** a night, especially during this initial start-up time as these new habits are being engrained.

- **Allow the transformation to be enjoyable.** Affirm it often. Tell yourself you are going from dowdy to Diva, from humdrum to "va va voom." From now on, describe yourself as fierce, fabulous, fit, fashionable, and full of life.

- **Switch your focus.** Ask "What do I do right?" instead of "What have I been doing wrong?"

- **Set up rewards for yourself**—something connected with reaching your goal, but not slippage. Get a facial or a massage—not a hot fudge sundae. Do small rewards. Big rewards are too far-reaching and take too long to reach. You want to reward yourself often.

- **Put one dollar in a jar every time you meet a goal** and when you get to $50, treat yourself.

- **Create a "Certificate of Appreciation of Yourself,"** and hang it where you can see it often.

- **Find meaningful work,** even if it is as a volunteer.

- **Get a pet** if you can handle the additional responsibility. If you are not ready for a pet, visit friends who have pets or children and play with them. Their simple joy is enlightening and inspiring.

- **Buy some plants,** plant a garden or just help something grow.

- **Develop your spirituality:** create a mantra, meditate or do yoga.

- **Laugh everyday.** Go to a stand-up comedy show: smile, laugh, grin (and bear it).

- **Visualize your dreams.** Start a dream scrapbook or dream journal. Hang pictures on the wall that represent your biggest goals.

- **Be optimistic.** Be honest. Don't fudge the numbers. Think about the habit you are trying to build, and don't compare yourself to others.

- **Forgive yourself,** and others—every day.

- **Put your attention on other people**. Get to know them, and see how you can contribute to their lives.

- **Just say "NO"** in order to stay on track.

- **Say "YES"** to new possibilities.

- **Get support**, Divas have an entourage—you should too! Join a group or start a group. Don't be a loner; surround yourself with positive and like-minded folks. Ask for help.

- **Do your best! Forget the rest.** Tomorrow is another day. Slow change is lasting change.

Take the Diva Pledge

By now I am sure you will agree being a Diva and building up your image power starts on the inside—it starts with self-care. Right now, make a commitment to yourself that you will from this day forward be a Diva!

To affirm your decision, I invite you to take this Diva Pledge as you improve your image through healthy self-care, and support your healthy self-care through improving your image.

- **Dress Like a Diva.** Start your day with doing your hair, makeup and having fun with fashion. There is a connection between your style and your soul that keeps manifesting all through the course of the day. Look like you care and the rest falls into place.

- **Dine Like a Diva.** Aim to be a better eater, not a perfect eater. Make vegetables the star of your meal. Use real china, placemats, a tablecloth, fresh flowers in a vase, goblets, silverware and cloth napkins at mealtime. And don't forget the candles!

- **Dance Like a Diva.** Movement is important to incorporate into daily health care. Thirty minutes of activity a day impacts diabetes positively by 58 percent. Move and groove!

- **Discuss Like a Diva.** You walk the walk—now talk the talk. Assemble an entourage, a group of likeminded, uplifting support team "fans" who give you credit for your positive efforts.

- **Decorate Like a Diva.** Surround yourself with comfort, beauty and organization that pleases your senses and elicits serenity.

- **Develop Your Diva-tude.** Stay informed and proactive about your health status. Educate yourself and then encourage those around you to do the same.

- **Devote Like a Diva.** Volunteer in your local community. Taking time to nurture family and friends and making a difference in someone's life can make a difference in your feelings of self-accomplishment.

+ **Do It Up Like a Diva.** Check your blood glucose, A1C, weight, blood pressure, cholesterol, but don't let the results determine your self-esteem. You are NOT your numbers. Go get a safe pedicure and examine your feet daily. Don't be hard on yourself and reward yourself for being you!

Image Building Resources for Women with Health Issues

Here are two major programs that you might find useful:

+ **"Look Good, Feel Better," program developed in 1989 by the Personal Care Products Council Foundation.** The Personal Care Products Council proved that transforming a woman's look during chemotherapy treatments also transformed her outlook. When the American Cancer Society and the National Cosmetology Association partnered together, they fulfilled the need to create an innovative program to help women maintain self-esteem and confidence in the face of cancer treatment and the appearance-related side effects which would invariably leave women feeling depressed and self-conscious. To their credit, it seemed obvious to connect the fact that helping women to feel feminine, attractive and beautiful after debilitating chemotherapy facilitated their recovery process. To find out more, visit www.lookgoodfeelbetter. org

+ **Divabetic: Makeover Your Diabetes.** Divabetic is a national nonprofit organization that infuses diabetes education with a "Glam More, Fear Less" philosophy, to help women at risk of, living with and affected by diabetes look at their health in new ways. We motivate individuals to live their best diabetes life. We strive to encourage prevention, early action and above all, education. Our mission revolves around community-inspired confidence.

Divabetic was inspired by the late R & B legend, Luther Vandross, and created and founded by his long-time assistant, Max Szadek. "Divabetic," a combination of the word 'diabetic' and the letter 'V' for Vandross, evokes feelings of power and positive attitude associated with the great DIVAS Luther loved like Ms. Patti LaBelle. We believe that if we empower the Diva within you to manage your diabetes properly, you will strive to live a healthy and full life. You may even feel glamorous! www.divabetic.org

CATHERINE SCHULLER, AICI CIP
Divabetic, Image & Style Advisor

(917) 375-0731
catherine@divabetic.org
www.divabetic.org

Based in New York City, Catherine is a former Ford model and well-known plus-size industry leader. Part consumer advocate, part promotions and marketing liaison, she is considered a consummate expert on the subject of "all things plus and full-figured." She serves as a media spokesperson and link between manufacturers, designers, retailers and the full-figured customer. Her clients have included major department stores as well as retail specialty stores. She is currently working on new campaigns and marketing efforts for clients within the burgeoning online plus size apparel industry.

Catherine is an inspirational and motivational icon who is often quoted in the fields of style and image. She has written numerous articles for major publications and newspapers and has appeared on several national and local morning talk shows including *The Today Show*, *The View*, *Neal Cavuto's Your World*, *CBS Evening News* and *The Early Show*. She was Fashion Retail Editor of *Mode* magazine and has had a line of clothing on QVC called *Shape Shopping*.

Catherine's passion for health, fashion, and beauty also led her to become a core team member and the image and style advisor of *Divabetic: Makeover Your Diabetes*, an outreach program that tours ten major cities in the United States each year and is sponsored by Novo Nordisk, targeting women living with, affected by or at risk for diabetes.

Find Your Unique Personal Style

Showcasing the Best Possible You

By Cheri Bertelsen, AICI CIP, CDI

Do you ever open your closet and feel it looks like six different people share it? It may be time to discover your personal style. Finding your unique personal style allows you to select garments and accessories that reflect your true self: the physical, emotional, and behavioral aspects that make you—*you*. Wearing your personal style lets your own unique beauty shine through and allows you to be noticed. You will feel more authentic and look great!

Amazing transformations occur when a client discovers her personal style. My client, Janice, worked in an environment where suits were required daily. When Janice wore a typical business suit, she never felt like it looked "right" on her. She came to me frustrated with her work wardrobe. Exploring Janice's personality and physical characteristics, we discovered Janice possessed a very strong affinity for femininity and beauty. Her menswear suits did not support the romantic trapped inside of her. We selected a few new suits for Janice, suits that consisted of a jacket and skirt, rather than pants. I remember the look on

Janice's face as she stepped out of the dressing room. With her tulip style skirt, she came out and twirled around like a little girl playing dress-up—she was radiant and full of life. For Janice, it just felt "right." We also traded her basic blouses for ones in soft colors. Teaming these with the suits she already owned and adding some appropriate jewelry pieces, Janice felt more at home in her old suits. Although we softened Janice's look, she maintained a very professional appearance and later reported back to me:

"For the first time, my work clothes feel like they belong to me and I have been experiencing a more positive response from my co-workers and clients. Maybe my attitude is better, or it could be the clothes—I don't know, I am not questioning it, I just know I love it!"

You can experience the benefits of finding and wearing your own unique personal style. Finding your personal style involves a three-step process:

- Identify your personality and physical design elements
- Investigate different style types
- Integrate your gathered knowledge with your lifestyle and goals

The first step of this process focuses on you: discovering things about your physical and emotional characteristics. First, you identify personality traits you possess and those perceived by others. Then, identify your physical design elements by looking closely at the coloring, form and lines found on your body. This personal examination will uncover things you may never have realized about yourself. During this process, allow yourself to explore freely without judgment or preconceived notions.

As you begin to investigate different style types you will become familiar with design elements intrinsically related to each style. You will learn that *dramatic* styling involves straight lines, bold colors and simple design, while *romantic* styling contains curved lines, soft colors and more complex design. Certain styles will resonate with the person inside of you, while others will sound like a blow horn.

Finally, you must combine all the information you have uncovered and integrate it with your lifestyle and goals. During this step, you will define your personal style and develop a wardrobe formula to use when you shop. Shopping and getting dressed will become a joy, rather than a struggle. If that sounds like something you have been waiting for, get started now and discover your unique personal style!

Identifying What Makes You—You

To find your personal style you must understand who you are, inside and out. Your personality qualities are just as important as your physical qualities when identifying your personal style. If you disregard discovering your personal and physical qualities and head right to investigating style types, you miss the *personal* element of personal style.

Discovering What Is Inside

It is time to discover the person inside of you. Make three photocopies of the list below. You will respond on one of the copies and give the others to a close friend and your spouse or significant other. If you would like more input, give additional copies to other friends or even a complete stranger. Circle all the words that describe you. Have others circle words they feel describe you. Go through the list quickly and stick with your first instinct. As you move through the list, remember that no words are better or worse than others; each word has its own unique value.

soft	striking	energetic	fun
dramatic	adventurous	artistic	avant-garde
unique	beautiful	serene	elegant
contemplative	comforting	hip	friendly
authoritative	credible	delicate	poised
dynamic	cute	extreme	relaxed
powerful	skillful	luscious	calm
exciting	carefree	free-spirit	tender
daring	confident	charming	compassionate
spicy	whimsical	original	gracious
dedicated	direct	innovative	reserved
playful	sultry	outrageous	unusual
discerning	animated	gentle	warm
composed	natural	sophisticated	controlled
polished	capable	sunny	athletic
cosmopolitan	flirtatious	imaginative	sensitive
dignified	dependable	enthusiastic	bold
mellow	free-spirited	caring	cultivated
reliable	outgoing	intense	trustworthy
optimistic	organized	peaceful	enticing

Now compile your list and the lists of those who helped with this exercise. Find the words common to all the lists. These words describe your personal qualities and personality traits. When you begin investigating style types, you will use these words to identify styles that are inherent to your personal qualities. It may be helpful to post these words where you can see them regularly: maybe on the bathroom mirror, your computer, or refrigerator. Identify the ones that feel like you. To get acquainted with her words, one of my clients even turned her words into a mantra she repeated out loud each morning, "I am elegant, I am serene, I am beautiful." Embrace the "you" inside!

One More Look Inside

Creating a portfolio of things you love can be an additional exercise to help discover the beauty inside of you. Create your portfolio by collecting pictures from magazines and catalogs. You may also find images from old greeting cards, calendars, postcards or even clipart. Your images may be of landscapes, animals, dinnerware, furniture, or flowers. Anything goes! Keep these images in a file folder or mount them in a scrapbook or photo album. You may even choose to incorporate them into a collage. This exercise could take days, months or even years, but start it now to begin identifying those things that speak to your heart.

Discovering What Is Outside

Now that we have taken a good look on the inside, let's identify some of your physical design elements. Circle the word following each physical characteristic that best describes your personal attributes.

- **Hair**: Straight, Curly, Wavy
- **Hair Color:** Very Light, Light, Medium, Dark, Very Dark
- **Eye Color**: Very Light, Light, Medium, Dark, Very Dark
- **Body Type**: Thin, Muscular, Athletic, Curvy
- **Height**: Very Short, Short, Average, Tall, Very Tall
- **Limb Lengths (Arm & Leg):** Short, Average, Long
- **Facial Features**: Rounded, Average, Angular
- **Personal Energy Level:** Serene, Relaxed, Average, Energetic, Intense

+ **Amount of Detail (or Design)**: Minimal, Moderate, Complex

(Minimal Detail = Straight, Smooth Hair, Solid Hair Color, Smooth Skin; Complex Detail= Curly Hair, Freckled Skin, Multi-Colored Hair)

At this point, you have gathered a large amount of information about yourself. Continue reviewing and becoming acquainted with this information as we move on to the second step in the process: investigating different style types.

Investigating Style Types

Over the years different stylists, image consultants and fashion experts have created several systems for categorizing garments and accessories based on each style's design elements. This has resulted in the average consumer having heard various names used to describe the same (or very similar) clothing style. Fortunately for the consumer, the name of a style has little significance as long as you understand the style elements characteristic to the style.

As William Shakespeare wrote, *"What's in a name? That which we call a rose by any other name would smell as sweet."*

This holds true for clothing styles as well. Whether you call it Classic, Traditional, or Town & Country, the style will still consist of conservative design, colors and fabrics. When working with clients, I choose to use the style words developed by a colleague of mine, Alyce Parsons. She developed the Universal Style System that consists of seven styles: Sporty, Traditional, Elegant, Feminine, Alluring, Creative, and Dramatic. Parsons has developed and meticulously tweaked her system for over 30 years. However, in addition to using Universal Style words, I enjoy sharing other experts' style names and allowing my client to choose the one that best suits her. After all, the description represents *her* unique personal style desire and is hers to own and embrace.

The following charts will give you a brief overview of style types. Although each chart starts with a style name from the *Universal Style System*, additional names are listed and may be a better "fit" for you. Pay attention to the design elements and message of each style type, looking for one or two that sound similar to things you have discovered about yourself.

SPORTY

Other Names	Sporty Natural, Casual, Athletic, Natural
Fabric Selection	Denim, cotton, natural fibers, slightly textured, crisp fabrics
Color Selections	Neutrals and bright colors. Wears several colors at a time.
Accessories	Practical—sports watch, small earrings, athletic shoes, backpack style purse, sunglasses, baseball cap
Makeup	Very natural
Hairstyle	Easy, carefree style
Line	Tailored; relaxed, rounded lines.
Design	More complex: lots of pockets, zippers, large buttons, rivets and flaps. Design allows for movement
Business Attire	Suit worn with crisp blouse and sporty colorful accessories
Messages Conveyed	Fun, relaxed, energetic, athletic, friendly, cute, carefree, whimsical, playful, warm, animated, natural, sunny, enthusiastic, outgoing, optimistic
Warning	May be difficult to project authority; may look underdressed or too casual
Other Variations	Gamine (Petite or Youthful Sporty) Preppy (athletic looking)

TRADITIONAL

Other Names	Classic, Town & Country, Soft Natural, Tailored
Fabric Selection	Solids, fine woolens, jersey, natural blends and fabrics; crisp, classic patterns
Color Selections	Traditional neutrals (beige, navy, gray) Traditional colors (blue, forest green, burgundy) Wears two to three colors in an outfit.
Accessories	Structured handbags, leather loafers, classic jewelry, cardigan sweater
Makeup	Natural looking, not overdone
Hairstyle	Neat and simple, classic styles
Line	Tailored, straight lines
Design	Functional clothing, menswear detailing, timeless quality, moderate amount of detail
Business Attire	Navy suit, soft-colored blouse, classic leather shoes, belt and handbag worn with classic jewelry
Messages Conveyed	Credible, authoritative, skillful, confident, dedicated, reserved, composed, controlled, capable, dependable, reliable, trustworthy, business-like, organized
Warning	May be perceived as old-fashioned or boring; possibly not a forward thinker
Other Variations	Preppy (academic looking)

ELEGANT

Other Names	Soft Classic, Classic Elegant, Refined
Fabric Selection	Fine fabrics, cashmere, silk, smooth surface
Color Selections	Soft colors, subtle neutrals, often wears all one color
Accessories	Fine classic pieces, pearls or semi-precious stones
Makeup	Conservative makeup applied to perfection. Always polished and put together.
Hairstyle	Soft and sleek
Line	Classic lines, softly tailored, formality, gracefulness and softness
Design	Minimal details—hidden zippers, buttons. Patterns tend to be tone-on-tone. Impeccable fit and tailoring.
Business Attire	Suit with graceful tailoring in soft neutral, may be skirt or trousers. Blouse in same color or shade of the suit. Fine, classic accessories.
Messages Conveyed	Serene, elegant, poised, confident, gracious, reserved, discerning, composed, polished, dignified, cultivated
Warning	May come across aloof or arrogant

FEMININE

Other Names	Romantic, Soft Gamine, Feminine Romantic, Supportive
Fabric Selection	Soft, flowing, smooth or slightly textured, lightweight, sheer.
Color Selections	Soft neutrals (white, ecru, light gray, dusty blue), soft colors and pastels. Enjoys wearing all one color or different values of one color. Soft multi-color prints, flowers and nature motifs in prints.
Accessories	Smaller, delicate detailing, jewelry with an heirloom quality, sweaters with soft airy quality, delicate shoes and purse.
Makeup	Dewy, soft looking, soft play on eyes and lips
Hairstyle	Long, soft curls, often hair is swept up in soft up-do
Line	Long, flowing lines, gentle-curved lines, soft details, rounded shoulders
Design	Intricate design, numerous details, rounded silhouette, no hard edges
Business Attire	Soft neutral suit with curved details—skirt or trousers. Light colored blouse or shell. Delicate shoes or pumps with feminine detailing. Jewelry has a light, feminine quality.
Messages Conveyed	Soft, beautiful, gracious, comforting, delicate, calm, tender, charming, compassionate, graceful, gentle, sensitive, caring, peaceful
Warning	May be difficult to wear this style effectively in a competitive workplace.
Other Variations	Ingenue, Soft Gamine (Petite or Young Romantic)

ALLURING

Other Names	Sexy, Glamorous, Theatrical Dramatic
Fabric Selection	Knits, Lycra, stretchy fabrics, smooth finishes, shiny, lightweight, tight leather
Color Selections	Neutrals (black and white), daring colors (red, hot pink, purple, emerald green, turquoise). Wears solids or prints with undulating design. Animal prints.
Accessories	S-curved shapes, oval and curved jewelry, Stiletto heels, strappy shoes and sandals, large hoop earrings. Simple design to not distract from the body
Makeup	Smoky eyes and glossy lips, sultry makeup
Hairstyle	Full hair, tousled hairstyles
Line	Body hugging lines, S-curved lines
Design	Minimal detail, form-fitting, nothing classic in detail
Business Attire	Black fitted suit with trousers or shorter straight skirt. Bright colored or appropriate animal print blouse or shell. High heel pumps and minimal jewelry.
Messages Conveyed	Luscious, exciting, daring, spicy, sultry, flirtatious, enticing, bold, direct, flashy
Warning	This style is difficult to use in a business setting. If it is your dominant personal style you must learn to use it appropriately in social situations.
Other Variations	Exotic (Alluring who wears tropical or scant resort wear)

DRAMATIC

Other Names	High Fashion, Trendy, Urban Chic, Dramatic-Striking
Fabric Selection	Firm fabrics that hold their shape, smooth fabrics, matte finish, closely woven, shiny
Color Selections	Neutrals (black and white), jewel tone colors (red, purple, magenta, sapphire, emerald), bright and intense, high contrast colors (black with white), one or two colors worn at a time, prints are geometric or abstract
Accessories	Jewelry pieces mimic geometric or abstract shapes, bold statement accessories, designer sunglasses, oversized handbag that makes a statement, smooth finishes
Makeup	Latest application, bold colors
Hairstyle	Very sleek and short, geometric cut, severe chignon or ponytail
Line	Slightly fitted to the body, exaggerated angles and shapes
Design	Minimal detail, non-classic, severely structured, geometric shapes, sleek
Business Attire	Black wool gabardine suit with asymmetrical closure. Accessorize with one bold piece of jewelry. Shoes or boots in the latest style.
Messages Conveyed	Striking, dramatic, avant-garde, hip, dynamic, extreme, powerful, direct, sophisticated, cosmopolitan, bold, intense
Warning	May appear remote or aloof. May be intimidating. Avoid looking overdone in certain social situations.

CREATIVE

Other Names	Arty, Offbeat, Art to Wear, Funky
Fabric Selection	Anything
Color Selections	Anything
Accessories	Anything
Makeup	Anything
Hairstyle	Anything
Line	Anything
Design	Anything
Business Attire	Suit with interesting styling or exaggerated silhouette, teamed with unexpected blouse or shell: interesting jewelry and shoes
Messages Conveyed	Adventurous, artistic, unique, outrageous, unusual, imaginative, free spirited
Warning	Difficult to wear in certain business situations.

The Creative style is difficult to define, because definition limits the possibilities available to the Creative. Forward-thinkers, they usually have tapped into a trend long before it becomes mainstream. The combinations worn by the Creative might appear as costumes on another style type, yet look completely appropriate on the Creative.

Studying the style charts, you may have discovered a style or two that resonate with you. Which styles' messages do you naturally communicate to those around you? Most likely you have personal words that fall under more than one style type. Which ones seem to be a reflection of who you are inside? Compare those styles to the personal portfolio of things you love. If you were to place your portfolio into one of the style categories, where would it best fit? Is it a combination of two or three? At this point your style list has narrowed. Now look at your physical characteristics and see where they fit into the style categories. Keep in mind different body types and features can be found in all the style types, but you can use your physical characteristics to break a tie or influence you towards one category or another.

You have taken the initial steps to discovering your unique personal style. Few individuals fall exclusively into one style type; rather they are a mixture of two or three types. Having a combination of style types allows you the choice of wearing the style appropriate for a particular occasion or situation.

Integrating Your Style Knowledge with Your Lifestyle and Goals

Like Janice, you may have discovered you have a Romantic locked inside of you, but in your workplace you need to project a professional, perhaps even powerful image. Many of my clients face this issue: finding the balance between their personal and public self. The resolution to this problem comes with the third step in our process, integrating the personal style knowledge you have gained with your current lifestyle and goals.

Think about your lifestyle. Would the personal style(s) you have identified be supportive of the different areas of your life— work, family, special interests, and recreation? For instance, the Romantic style supports the role of a teacher, counselor, wife or mother—but is not the best choice for a high-powered attorney. The Sporty may come across as too casual running an art gallery.

She may want to implement elements of the Dramatic, Creative or Elegant style to look appropriate when at work.

Think about your goals. Do the style(s) you identified assist you in reaching those goals? Maybe you have discovered that you are a Dramatic. At your workplace, this style allows you to be powerful and commanding. However, socially you may want to date more. Powerful and commanding may not be the best approach when trying to attract that special someone! Working in a very conservative office environment, your Traditional style works perfectly for you, but you have the desire to change careers and work in a more creative field. Interviewing for the new job will call for you to down play some traditional messages and allow your creative self to be seen.

Now that you possess the knowledge of different style types, you can adapt elements into your own unique style to create the effect you desire. For example, if you have discovered you are a Sporty, but need to be perceived as being more powerful in the workplace, borrow some of the characteristics of the Dramatic style. You may limit the amount of colors you wear to one or two. You may choose to wear higher contrast in your garments. Or you may choose to limit the amount of accessories worn at work. On the weekends and evenings you can "sport" it up, wear as many colors as you want—but adapt your style to be effective while at work.

We have come to the defining moment. Finding your unique personal style takes place when you contemplate your lifestyle and goals, while considering the styles that resonate with you. This is the moment you become an Urban-Chic Romantic or Funky, Refined Traditionalist. Play with it and see what you discover to be your unique personal style.

Using Your Unique Personal Style

How does the Urban-Chic Romantic dress? She creates her wardrobe formula by choosing the elements she closely identifies with from each of her styles. This could mean she wears black and white, but softens her look with heirloom styled jewelry in an antiqued, textured silver. Or maybe she wears a black turtleneck, trousers and boots, softened with an airy black angora shawl, and chandelier earrings.

It may seem a bit overwhelming to develop your own wardrobe formula. Consider these guidelines before hitting the stores:

- **Pare it down to three.** Success developing your wardrobe formula will come when you identify with three styles or less. Most of us have a little of each style within us, but work hard to find those that truly express who you are.

- **Shop in your closet first.** My clients have found the most success implementing their unique personal style after cleaning out their closet. Keep items that belong to your style(s) and get rid of anything that does not.

- **Buy basics in the Sporty, Traditional or Elegant Style.** According to Alyce Parsons, the Sporty, Traditional and Elegant styles make the best building blocks for your wardrobe. Buy basic core pieces, such as jackets, trousers, and skirts in one of these three styles.

- **Make a list.** I like to have a list of my client's words with me when we go shopping. When selecting a garment it must pass the litmus test of her words before we make the purchase. You can also run the purchase by your personal style name—"*Is this really Funky, Refined Traditionalist?*"

You have a wardrobe formula ready to be discovered. It is unique to you and truly reflects your personality. It will allow those around you to see the unique beauty you possess. Discover your unique personal style and build a wardrobe that resonates with YOU!

CHERI BERTELSEN, AICI CIP, CDI

It's not about changing an image ...it's about changing a life!

(559) 260-8161
cheri@cbcolorandimage.com
www.cbcolorandimage.com

Cheri is based in Fresno and Pebble Beach, California and serves quite a diverse audience of clients. Her clients include professionals involved in marketing, healthcare, sports, agriculture, education, training, residential construction, and recent students entering the work force. Cheri has served as a conference presenter for such groups as Kaiser Permanente, the California Association of Nurse Practitioners and the Association of Image Consultants International (AICI). Working with businesses, she presents workshops and seminars on business dress and etiquette and has helped companies establish dress code policies in the workplace. She also works with individuals, assisting them with color and style analysis, closet audits, and personal shopping. Cheri has completed extensive color and style training through Colour Designers International (CDI). As an added benefit to her image clients, Cheri has trained with both The Coaches Training Institute (CTI) and the Career Coach Academy.

Working with both groups and individuals, Cheri incorporates her skills in color analysis, image consulting and coaching to give her clients the "complete" package." Her energetic, engaging manner makes her presentations non-threatening, informative, and fun!

Embrace Your Body Shape to Enhance Your Image

Learn How to Select Clothing That Flatters Your Unique Body Shape

By Elaine Stoltz, AICI CIM

Have you ever looked in the mirror and felt dissatisfied with your reflection? As a woman, it is easy to assume that there is something wrong with your body when you are frustrated with your appearance. Thoughts such as, "I am too fat," "My hips are too big," or "My legs are too short" race through your head.

There is nothing wrong with your body; you just need to learn how to dress for your distinctive body shape. Clothes are typically created around the size, shape, and proportion of a model's body. Since not every woman belongs on a runway, and because we are not all the same shape, it is unrealistic for us to expect to all look fabulous in the same styles and shapes of clothes. To worsen the problem, women's sizing is not consistent across clothing lines. For example, a size 10 in one clothing line might be a size 8 in another line, and a size 12 in yet a different line. The way clothes are made can often cause them to be ill-fitting and look unflattering.

The good news is that there is hope for you! By embracing your body shape and learning how to dress and shop for your unique body, clothing yourself can become fun again. Not only will you put an end to frustrating shopping experiences, you will learn to love the reflection you see in the mirror and others will definitely notice how fantastic you look.

Body Silhouette

When you walk into a room, people see you at a distance. Even from 30 feet away, you are immediately recognized by the outside shape (or silhouette) of your body. People will notice the general size of your body first. How large or small is your body shape? Are you tall or short? Are you heavy or thin? The female body, unlike the male body, can take on a variety of shapes. Our bone structure is the internal core that determines our body shape. While some women have wide shoulder bones, others may have wide pelvic bones. We cannot change our bone structure. Therefore, we must learn to love our body and dress to enhance our assets while camouflaging our areas of concern.

As an image consultant, no one ever asks me to make them appear shorter and fatter. They always want to look taller and thinner. In order to produce long and lean shapes, you need to create optical illusions by using vertical lines. Vertical lines always make you look taller, while horizontal lines make you appear shorter. Every horizontal line in an outfit shortens you by two inches. One client that I had worked with on a Body Shape Analysis later told me that people are always asking her now if she has lost weight because of the way she has learned to use vertical lines to enhance her body shape.

Determine Your Body Shape

With 20 years of experience in image consulting, I have found that all of my clients fit into one of six body silhouettes: Hourglass, Contoured Rectangle, Rectangle, Oval, Triangle, and Inverted Triangle. In order to determine your body shape, you must do a little bit of work. Create the drawing of your body silhouette by following the instructions below:

1. Take a picture of yourself wearing a formfitting, one-piece swimsuit or leotard with your arms extending from the side of your body at a 45-degree angle.
2. Enlarge and print the photo on a sheet of paper.
3. With a pen, draw along the side of your body from the tip of your shoulder, cutting in across your arm, down past your waist, and extending to your thigh.

This creates your body silhouette. Once you have drawn your silhouette, you are ready to determine your body shape.

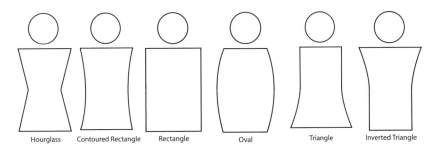

Hourglass Contoured Rectangle Rectangle Oval Triangle Inverted Triangle

Dress for Your Body Shape

Hourglass. When we visualize the ideal female shape, we typically think about the Hourglass figure. Marilyn Monroe's figure is a great example of this shape with her small waist, full bust, and shapely hips. Many current celebrities, like Scarlett

Johannson, fit into the Hourglass classification with their shapely figures. Looking at the drawing of your body silhouette, determine if your waist seems small in comparison to your bust and hips. If you are an Hourglass, then your bust or shoulders are the same width as your hips. The upper and lower half of your body will look balanced. In order to accent your best features, you should always show your waist. Do not wear gunnysacks or t-shirts hanging straight from your bust. These tops will make you look at least ten pounds heavier because they hide your small waist. Show off your figure by wearing dresses with waists, and use belts often.

Contoured Rectangle. The Contoured Rectangle is a shape halfway between an Hourglass and a true Rectangle. Look at the drawing of your body silhouette. Does the line indent at the waist, but it does not indent enough to look like an Hourglass? When women reach menopause, the waist seems to expand no matter how thin you are. This may cause an Hourglass to transform into a Contoured Rectangle. If you are a Contoured Rectangle, then your bust or shoulders are still in proportion with your hips. Cameron Diaz's figure is a Contoured Rectangle. While she is very slender and her waist is smaller than her shoulders and hips, her waist is not small enough to classify her as an Hourglass. The key point to enhancing your shape as a Contoured Rectangle is to always create an outfit that has a semi-fitted shape through the waistline, but you should never, ever wear a belt. A Contoured Rectangle should leave it to the observer's imagination to decide the size of the waist. Wearing a jacket or blouse that has darts will contour the waist without calling attention to it. As a Contoured Rectangle, your waist should never be the focal point of your outfit.

Rectangle. The Rectangle does not have a waist. Look at the drawing of your body silhouette. Is the line from your shoulders past your bust and waist to your hips a straight line or very close to a straight line? Are your bust and hips close to the same width? Then you are a Rectangle. You will look great in straight garments that flow through your angular body. Coco Chanel, a Rectangle, hated the fashions that cinched in at the waist and created full skirts over curvy hips. Those fashions did not flatter her body shape. Instead, she wore menswear-inspired clothing that was a natural extension of her body shape and provided her with balance. She loved her straight shirts and jackets over a straight skirt or pants. Belts did not exist in her closet. Instead, she created focal points above the bust line to draw the eye upward. Diane Keaton is an example of a Rectangle that utilizes Coco Chanel's body shape concepts. Keaton wears drapable fabrics, oftentimes menswear-inspired suiting, which flow freely over her body.

Oval. The Oval, sometimes referred to as the Apple, has a larger waist than her bust and hips. Look at the drawing of your body silhouette. Does your line curve out from the body further at the waist than at the bust and hips, or does it appear that the abdomen is coming forward in front? Aretha Franklin's figure is an example of an Oval with the majority of her weight carried in the front of her body, similar to a woman that is pregnant, while her hips appear narrower than her waist.

An Oval looks fabulous in flared jackets or dresses. Drape the garment from your shoulders and let the fabric flow loosely over your torso in order to create a swinging silhouette. On the upper half of your body, whether you wear a jacket or blouse, the clothing should extend to your hip and cover the waist area. A layered look is quite flattering on the Oval. Wear a non-knit shell, such as silk or polyester, with an open blouse or jacket layered over it. This creates an elongated torso that will not cling to the body. Always wear a straight skirt or tapered pants. If you enjoy wearing dresses, keep them knee-length and avoid mid-calf or ankle-length dresses. The dress should drape from the shoulders and flow loosely over the torso. Drapable, rather than stiff, fabric looks best on the Oval. Do not forget to show off your great legs.

Triangle. The Triangle, sometimes referred to as the Pear, is the most common female body shape. Think about performer Beyoncé Knowles' figure. The hips or thighs appear to be the widest area of the body when compared to the bust and waist. These women are built with wide pelvic bones for childbearing. An Hourglass shaped woman may gain weight first in her hips and thighs, thus converting her to a Triangle. Look at the drawing of your body silhouette. Does the silhouette line curve widest at the hip or thigh area? If so, then you are a Triangle.

Does the silhouette line from the shoulders to the waist curve in toward the waist, or does the line go straight down or outward? The size of your waist may vary from small to full. There are two types of Triangles: the first has a smaller waist than the bust and the second has a waist that is the same width or wider than the bust.

If you are a Triangle with a small waist, then create an optical illusion that makes you look like a Contoured Rectangle. You should wear semi-fitted jackets, sweaters, blouses, or tops. Do not cinch in the waist with a belt, but create volume on the upper half of your body by wearing light, rather than dark, colors and shoulder pads. Wear darker colors on the bottom. The hem of your tops should fall below the hip line when wearing pants. A flared, swing skirt will also help to camouflage the hip area.

If your waist is the same width as your bust, then create an optical illusion that makes your shape look like a Rectangle. Once again, to balance the lower half of the body with the upper half, wear light colors on the top half of the body and dark colors on the bottom. Wearing shoulder pads will also help give the illusion of a Rectangular shape. Select soft, drapable fabrics for your jackets, blouses, tops, and dresses. The shape should be straight or slightly flared from the shoulder. You should not wear a belt, but let the lower edge of the jacket or top fall below the hip line. Straight pants or skirts will also look great on you.

Inverted Triangle. The Inverted Triangle's bust or shoulders are wider than her hips. Picture Serena Williams with her broad, athletic shoulders and slim hips. A woman with very wide shoulders, such as a swimmer, is an Inverted Triangle. Another type of Inverted Triangle is a woman who wears a DD or larger bra. The focal point of this woman is the full bust, which can make her quite self-conscious. Her hips are narrower than her bust or shoulders. Look at the drawing of your body silhouette. Does your silhouette line appear the widest on the upper half of your figure? If so, then you are an Inverted Triangle.

You will most likely either have a small waist with slightly wider hips or a torso that is fairly straight from the bust down. If you are the first type of Inverted Triangle with a small waist and slightly wider hips, then you should create a semi-fitted look by wearing a flared skirt with soft, moveable fabric to balance the upper half of your body. If you are the second type of Inverted Triangle with a torso that is almost straight from the bust down, then you should wear clothing that is straight through the waist, hip, and leg area. The full-busted women should wear open jackets or blouses that create a strong vertical line on the upper half of the body.

Body Proportion

Do you find that most clothes off the rack do not fit your body perfectly? Are clothes always too long for you? Are they too short? There is nothing wrong with your body. Clothing in stores is cut for a balanced body length proportion that may not be the same as yours.

You need to be aware of your proportion so that you can dress accordingly. What is your body proportion?

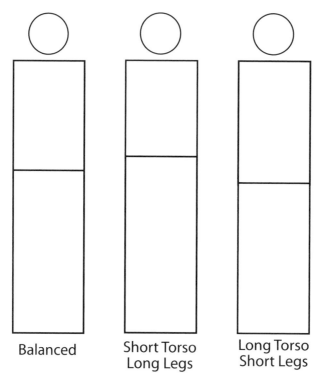

Balanced   Short Torso   Long Torso
                    Long Legs   Short Legs

To determine your body proportion, measure your height and divide it in half. If the halfway mark is at the hipline, then you are balanced. If your body's halfway mark is anywhere else, then you have unbalanced body proportion.

If you are balanced from head to toe, you do not have to concern yourself with proportion. If your torso is longer than your legs, then you want to create the illusion that your legs are longer. Wearing high heels and short skirts will help. Do not wear cropped pants because they will only make you look shorter.

If your legs are longer than your torso, then you want to create the illusion that your torso is longer. Wear long jackets, and do not tuck your tops in at the waist, but let them flow over your waist to your hips, so you appear to have more length in the upper half of your body. You should also wear boot-cut or wide-legged pants. Tapered pants will only make your legs appear longer.

By adjusting your clothing according to the proportion of your body, your body will appear balanced and more pleasing to the eye.

Commit to Change

Dressing your body shape is not a simple process, and the techniques outlined above can take a great deal of time and energy to master. This chapter only summarizes the basic guidelines for dressing. If you would like further information and instruction, seek the services of an image consultant. Many image consultants offer services that explain detailed guidelines for the style of garments most flattering for your specific body shape. Image consultants are trained in body shape and style and will provide an expert opinion on what clothing styles look best on you. It is often easy to develop a personal bias toward our bodies; therefore, seeking the services of an image consultant can help you to objectively identify your body shape and determine the styles of clothing that will accent your best body features.

An image consultant will also leave no aspect of dress up for interpretation. You will be able to shop easily by looking at the garment on a hanger and immediately determine if it should be taken into your dressing room. After her Body Shape Analysis, one of my clients said, "I can now focus when I go in a store and quickly see if there is anything for my body shape. By looking at the clothing item on the hanger, I know whether or not it will work for me, and I no longer waste time or money when shopping."

Learning to master correct proportion and making great clothing choices can be challenging, but the results of your hard work and efforts are sure to pay off. "I feel great about myself every day when I walk out the door," said one of my clients. Another client said, "Completing the Body Shape Analysis was the best money that I ever spent. Knowing the styles of clothing that are perfect for my body has saved me time and money when shopping, and I can feel guilt-free about discarding clothing that does not flatter my shape."

Commit to dressing for your body shape, and you will look and feel fabulous. You will love the way you look, receive many compliments, and find that shopping can actually be both fun and successful.

ELAINE STOLTZ, AICI CIM
Stoltz Image Consulting, Inc.

Make a great first impression!

(817) 924-8300
elaine@stoltzimage.com
www.stoltzimage.com

Elaine Stoltz is the founder and President of *Stoltz Image Consulting, Inc.*, a personal image consulting firm located in Fort Worth, Texas. She is a Certified Image Master, one of seven in the world, calling herself "an architect of the body" and specializing in individual nonverbal communication. Elaine started her image consulting business in 1989, concentrating on positive first impressions. She works with both individuals and businesses, and has helped thousands of clients, both men and women, find their unique style while enhancing their self-confidence and credibility. Her individual services include color analysis, body shape analysis, closet audits, personal shopping, and cosmetic makeovers.

Elaine is a highly sought after speaker and trainer for many national corporations and has been quoted and featured in radio, TV, magazines, and newspapers.

Elaine has been instrumental in advancing the field of image consulting. The Stoltz Image Institute trains students in developing and maintaining a successful image consulting business.

Elaine has served as International President, Vice President of Certification and Treasurer of the Association of Image Consultants International, and in 2002 she received the association's Award of Excellence.

Master the Power of Color

Use Color to Your Advantage in Your Business and Personal Life

By Bernie Burson, AICI FLC, CDI

How would you like to be perceived at work? Do you want to be seen as a team player? Is it important to appear credible and trustworthy? Do you need to look authoritative? Your color choices will help you create the effect you want to have on others.

Color is a powerful tool. Studies have shown that people have both a physical and a psychological reaction to color. Colors can be energizing or calming, both to the viewer and to the wearer. Color can make you appear formal and powerful, or friendly and approachable. However, for the best effect, the colors you wear must work well with one another—and with you.

Colors appear in different qualities. Here are a few terms that can help you understand how colors work:

+ **Pure colors** are bright and intense, like artists' paint right out of the tube. These colors are high energy. Think of bright apple red, broccoli green, and tangerine orange.

- **Tinted colors** have had a lot of white added, so appear lighter and more pastel. They have a softer, gentler feel to them. Like ice cream flavors strawberry, pistachio, and lemon sherbet.

- **Shaded colors** have had black added, so they are very dark. Because of this, shaded colors can often serve as neutrals. They also add formality and authority. Think of a deep rich purple, navy blue or espresso brown.

- **Muted or toned colors** have been altered by adding gray (creating a cooler tone), or by adding brown (creating a warmer tone), or by adding the color's complement—its opposite on the color wheel—to create a softer version of the original color without making it warmer or cooler. Unless you have very dark skin, or very fair skin and black hair, toned or muted colors will work best for you. Also, toned colors tend to be more appropriate in a business setting. Raisin, paprika, moss green, and French blue are examples of muted colors.

Easy Guide to Creating Effects with Color

Now that you have some basic terminology, let's look at the effects you can achieve with specific colors or color combinations:

To Appear:	Wear:
Credible, capable, professional, trustworthy	Navy blue, medium to dark gray
Dependable, reliable	Medium to dark brown, navy blue
Serious, authoritative	Black, charcoal, black alternative
Refined, elegant	Burgundy, dark purple, pearl gray, white, or all one toned color
Friendly, approachable	Beige, peach, medium blue, light colors in combination, prints
Creative, with fresh ideas	Green, purple, pink, but not blue or gray
Powerful, assertive	Red, red-black-white, any combination of very dark and very light colors, but not a print
Low-key, non-threatening	Light to medium gray, soft colors, especially pale pink
Cheerful, highly visible	Yellow, but be careful; it's a tricky color to wear – it has to be the right one for you
Attention-getting	Bright colors, preferably as a blouse or accent piece, not an entire suit or dress; or high-contrast combinations with a pop of accent color
Energetic	Lots of red, or orange in smaller amounts; avoid orange in conservative environments

Another concept to learn is contrast, which refers to the relative lightness or darkness, known as the "value," of adjacent colors. Black and white is a high-contrast combination, as is dark navy and pale yellow, or espresso brown and cream. As noted in the chart, this combination has a powerful, assertive effect. It's great to wear in the boardroom or whenever you need to show authority.

A high-contrast color combination draws more attention than a low-contrast combination. Be aware that the eye is drawn to the area where the dark and light colors meet. For example, if you wear a white or very light-colored jacket with black or dark-colored pants, you draw attention to your hipline, where the jacket ends. For clients who want to camouflage the hip area, I recommend they keep tops and bottoms close to the same value.

Another way to attract attention is to wear a bright color with black or another dark neutral. Again, the eye will be drawn to the junction of the two colors, so be careful how you use this combination. For business, bright colors should be worn in small amounts as an accent to a more toned or neutral-colored suit or dress.

Making It Personal

Before you run out and stock your wardrobe according to the above chart, there's another aspect to consider: color harmony. Not only must your color combinations look well together, everything you wear should harmonize with your personal coloring.

Anybody can do a red-black-white combination in an effort to send the power message. To ensure that you get the message across, the power combination has to have the *right* red and white for you. To find those, and to create the next set of effects, you need to have a personal color analysis that gives you a palette of your skin tones—both beige and blush tones, hair colors, eye-related colors, and your versions of red and white, along with several other colors that harmonize with your personal or body colors. Many of the authors of this book are highly qualified color designers who can assist with this process.

Using Body Colors

+ **Wear your eye-related color when you want to appear sincere, honest, believable, and trustworthy.** This is an excellent color to wear if you're in sales. When you wear your eye color near your face—in a blouse, scarf, jacket or necklace and earrings using semi-precious stones—people are almost forced to look into your eyes. It's that eye connection that conveys the feeling of believability and trust.

+ **Wear skin tones, alone or in combination with similar-value colors, to seem non-threatening, friendly and approachable.** Skin tones and light, bright colors are great to wear if you're working with children. An added bonus: skin tones make you look rested and fresh. I always recommend that clients wear skin-tone blouses or shells with suits instead of white. Pure white is not very kind to your complexion, and if you have problem skin, bright white will make it look worse.

+ **Wearing a suit in creamy ivory and a blouse in your blush skin tone will give you a lovely and delicate look.** This is great if you want people to open doors for you or let you go ahead of them in line. This is *not* the combination to wear when you need to project authority or ask for a raise.

+ **If your hair color is blonde or light-to-medium brown, use your hair color as your light neutral.** This shade is also an excellent choice for shoes and handbags. Gray is often promoted as a light neutral, but finding the right shade of gray can be difficult, especially for those with warm skin tones.

Black, or a Black Alternative?

If you have—or used to have—black or very dark brown hair, you probably look great in black. If your hair color is lighter, chances are good that black will not be as wonderful on you. In that case, your color designer will give you some "black alternatives." These are very dark versions of your best colors, and are usually dark enough to be worn with black belts and shoes. My black alternatives are dark neutral brown, dark teal, and a very dark hunter green. All of these coordinate well with my skin-tone colors and the lighter colors on my palette.

Depending on their personal coloring, I've given clients such black alternatives as midnight blue, deep purple and very dark burgundy or maroon. As with black, all black alternatives, when worn alone or with just a touch of color, send the message of stately elegance and authority.

An Advisory

If you have very dark hair and know you look terrific in black, be advised: Even though you look wonderful, you still look intimidating in black. That's great—if that's your goal. If not, consider another choice. One of my clients is a physician and department head at a large hospital. She's also single and wants to date. She has very dark hair, so I advised her to avoid wearing black on a first date. It's way too intimidating, especially given her profession. A rosy skin tone, which is very romantic, would be a good choice, as would one of the bright colors she looks so good in. Even a dark brown would be preferable—especially because it's her eye color. However, when this client needs to be the person in control of a meeting, a black suit accented with a red blouse, pin or scarf will do the trick.

More Color Power Tips

+ **Wear your version of red when you want to appear confident, dramatic, exciting, and powerful.** Wearing your red can also give you an energy boost, but make sure you're prepared for it; if you're under a lot of stress, red can make you feel even more tense. Wear blue-greens if you need to de-stress.

+ **A softer version of your red can be very appealing to men.** Use this power wisely! If you wear red to the office, be sure that your clothing is not too tight or the slightest bit revealing, as that would definitely send a message inappropriate for the workplace. And red doesn't need that kind of help. It can do the job on its own.

+ **With light-colored clothing, or to make your legs look longer, wear shoes in a color close to your beige skin tone.** This is a much better choice than white shoes, which will draw attention to your feet. If you watch "Dancing with the Stars" on television, you'll notice that the female dancers almost always wear skin-tone shoes, regardless of the color of their dance costumes.

+ **If your body colors are all neutral (black, brown, beige), you not only look great in neutrals, you're able to wear a wide range of colors.** You can also usually get away with wearing some of the more intense hues. I would still advise using bright colors in moderation for office attire.

+ **If you have red or blonde hair, and blue, green, or hazel eyes, wearing all neutral colors would not be your best**

choice. Wear neutrals—just be sure to add some color with a blouse, scarf or colorful jewelry. Because you are colorful to begin with, you'll also look wonderful when you wear colors in combination, such as deep purple with a soft pink, or sage green with peach.

✦ **White is not your friend.** As you may have gathered from earlier comments, I am not a big fan of pure white. Many people think it's a neutral; it's not. White is brighter than the brightest color and will stand out emphatically against other colors. It will also make your teeth look yellow by comparison. My color clients always receive a *version* of white that harmonizes with their teeth and the whites of their eyes.

The Added Power of Personal Colors

Wearing your personal colors is more important than choosing colors for their impact or effect. If a particular color or color combination makes you look pasty, tired or ill, it can negate the effect you're trying to achieve. If I wore navy blue and pure white in an effort to look capable and dependable, it would likely backfire because I would also look pale and tired. "Dependably tired" would not be a helpful effect. But I could wear a teal navy suit with an ivory or skin-tone blouse and look capable, dependable, *and* radiantly healthy—a much more powerful and positive impression.

If you are dubious about personal color analysis because you had your colors done 20 years ago and didn't really like all the colors in the pre-made packet you were given, take another look. Most of today's professional color designers will choose a palette for you that includes your body colors—skin tones and hair and eye colors—as well as a selection of neutrals, brights, and subdued colors that will make you look wonderful.

Even if you were lucky enough to have had a personalized color analysis in the '80s, you're due for an update. As we mature, our skin tone changes and our hair gets grayer, or turns a completely different color—with assistance. Chances are, you don't look as wonderful in the bright colors you used to love so much, and you'll need to look for more toned versions of those colors. I point out to clients that toned colors are more sophisticated and rich looking than the pure pigment colors. Toned colors convey more authority while clear, overly bright colors are usually associated with children.

I'll say it again: the best way to ensure that you look fabulous in the colors you wear is to have a personal color analysis by a professional color designer. People react more favorably to you when you present a harmonious appearance, and when you know you look good, it really boosts your feelings of power and confidence.

Putting It All Together

Once you have your personal color palette, you're on your way to a new system of dressing. To assemble a working wardrobe that will allow you to create several different effects:

+ Start with three basic, unembellished suits—or coordinating jackets, pants, and skirts. One can be in black or your favorite black alternative, one in a light neutral such as beige, gray or taupe, and one in the medium-value color that harmonizes with the most colors on your palette. For me, that color is bronze green, my eye-related color.

+ Next, get shells or blouses in your beige and blush skin tones, your shade of white, your version of red, and your eye-related colors. You may also wish to have blouses or twinsets in some of your other palette colors.

+ Finally, select shoes in dark and light neutrals, a neutral handbag, a few colorful pins, and scarves, and perhaps a signature necklace in one of your key colors, preferably your eye-related color.

With this wardrobe and the above guidelines, you will be able to appear authoritative, or credible, or approachable, or elegant, or dramatic—whenever you choose. By incorporating body colors and dressing harmoniously and strategically, you will **master the power of color!**

BERNIE BURSON, AICI FLC, CDI

Discover your personal power through image.

(541) 344-4957
bb@bernieburson.com
www.bernieburson.com

Bernie began her career as an image consultant learning the importance of color. She has studied extensively with some of the industry's leading color experts, is now a certified color designer and holds the designation of CDI (Certified Color Designer). She counsels professionals on the use of color and the powerful non-verbal message it sends. Among her many clients, Bernie enjoys working with law firms to help them project the best image in court cases. She advises attorneys and their clients on styles to choose or avoid in specific situations. In an all-important case where people are determining a person's future, image plays a critical role.

Bernie is a past president of Colour Designers International, was on the Board of the San Francisco Bay Area Chapter of AICI, the Association of Image Consultants International, from 2002 to 2007, and is AICI's International Vice President Member Communications for 2007–2009. Now located in Eugene, Oregon, Bernie specializes in personal color design for individuals and is a sought-after presenter of training programs on appropriate business attire and other aspects of appearance, behavior, and communication.

Foundation Pieces

The Secret Behind Every Beautiful Curve

By Bianca Stark-Falcone, AICI FLC

The appearance of your clothes and how they look on you can only be as good as the foundation pieces that give them support from underneath. What happens underneath the dress makes a dramatic effect on how the dress appears to others! Imagine that perfect outfit: a beautiful pair of trousers, perhaps with a gorgeous silk sweater, but lumps and bumps and bulging lines appear where they shouldn't. What should sit underneath your beautiful clothes are smooth beautiful curves. No outfit looks its best without the right foundation pieces—your undergarments!

The wrong undergarments, even on a perfect body, can make the clothes lying over them look awkward. The right undergarments, however, even on a body that's less than perfect, can make those clothes look amazing. Let's face it ladies, very few of us think that we have a perfect body. We all can use a little extra help to look our best.

Finding the right clothes that fit your body well is half the battle; the other half is supporting those perfect clothes correctly. "Badly fitting underwear will make for badly fitting outfits every time."

The correct bra can make you look ten years younger, producing the same effect as surgery for thousands of dollars less. The right underwear will create a smooth, often supportive surface for your rear while shape wear can smooth, flatten, tone, and even reduce you a size! You will look and feel your best when your clothes fit your body right, but your clothes will only look as good as the undergarments allow them to look. A good foundation will make you feel your best. It will help you feel confident, sexy, and even more capable.

The All Important Bra

The bra is the one foundation piece that is the most simple to change, yet has the most dramatic effect on the way your clothes look on your body. Most women don't know as much about bras as they should. In fact, most women have no idea what bra size they truly are! Ask any lingerie sales women and they will tell you that most of their customers wear the wrong size bra or have no idea what size they are at all. Wearing the correct bra size and finding the right style for your body can make all the difference. For the bra to accentuate all the right curves, it must fit! The wrong bra can ruin the appearance of an otherwise amazing top; the right bra can make an otherwise plain top make *you* look amazing!

A note here to those with a more petite bust size: you may think that the bra topic does not apply to you, that you do not really need to wear a bra. Well, you are wrong. The right bra is still going to support and define your subtle curves, making them look their best.

I highly recommend having a professional fit you. Most of the higher end department stores will have lingerie specialists trained to measure you correctly. If you don't have a good experience at first, please persist and try again. Good fit and comfort are worth the effort.

If you prefer, you can measure your bra size yourself. Here's how:

+ To measure your band size: use a soft measuring tape and place it around your back and under your arms so that the tape comes all the way around your torso and lies on the top part of your bust. The number you get should be even, if it's odd, add 1" to the number.

+ To measure your cup size, loosely measure all the way around the fullest part of your bust. The difference between your bust measurement and your band measurements tells you your cup size. If the difference is: 1"= A cup, 2"= B cup, 3"= C cup, 4"= D cup, 5"=DD and so on.

Measuring for the fit of a bra really is as much of an art as it is a science. Remember that your cup size can vary, depending on brand and style. Different styles are going to fit each body differently. Don't assume that because a bra is your size it will automatically be the right bra for you. The most important thing about a bra is that it fits correctly. Here is where a knowledgeable sales woman can be very helpful.

Remember that bras stretch out. When you first purchase a new bra, you should start by fitting it on the loosest hook so as it stretches, you can tighten it. You may also need to adjust the straps of the bra. In fact you are supposed to; that is why they are adjustable. I am always amazed by how many women ignore this particular feature of a bra. They are so surprised when I do this simple adjustment for them, and even more surprised by how much more perky they look with just this small tweak.

A bra should fit and feel good. The straps should not pull, or bag, or bulge. Your breasts should feel snug and supported in the cups. Your breasts should also be elevated and perky if your bra is doing its job correctly. If your bra is too big, it will be unsupportive and feel saggy. It is almost pointless to bother wearing a bra that no longer supports you. Bras will wear out. So if a bra, even one that used to make you look amazing, is not doing its job anymore, then it is time to retire it.

A bra that is too tight is just as bad. Bulging out is unacceptable. Extra bumps above, below or on the sides are unflattering and it means your bra is definitely too small. You cannot squeeze a C cup into a B cup bra, just like you cannot fit a full-sized sheet onto a queen-sized mattress. It simply does not work!

Can you recognize and name the different parts of a bra? Examine and evaluate these elements of construction when adding to your bra selection:

+ **The back wings:** the size and stiffness of this part of the bra will affect the level of support the bra will give you. The back wings for a C or D cup should be wider with at least three rows of hooks.

+ **The straps:** the thickness of the straps will also affect support level. If you carry a lot of pressure on your shoulders due to a large cup size, you might look for padded shoulder straps. You can also purchase gel inserts for your shoulders separately and wear with any bra.

+ **The center gore:** is the triangular piece that attaches the two cups. If you want more support or fuller coverage, this piece should be larger and longer. It should also be made of a stiffer, stronger material. A smaller center gore is going to give less coverage and allow for more cleavage to show. This can be useful for a sexier, lower cut neckline.

- **Construction of the cup** is also important to notice. Again, the thicker, stronger, and stiffer the material, the more supportive the bra will be. Lightly padded cups are often more supportive than a cup made out of a single layer of material like a spandex cotton or lace blend.

- **The underwire or inner sling:** The underwire design offers more support because it gives the bra more structure, but it is not always comfortable for every woman. The inner sling has a second layer of fabric that curves around the bottom of the cup for added support. It is a good alternative and can often be as supportive as the underwire, and is much more comfortable.

Understanding the different types of bras and the silhouette that they help you create will also help you make a more educated bra purchase:

- **A minimizer** will flatten you out a bit, but hold you in well and does wonders to help you contain your curves.

- **A molded bra** is often supportive and comfortable and helps you show off your curves. It is constructed with the curves of the cup molded into the material. It is made of thicker foam-like material, without adding extra bulk, so it is supportive, smooth and also helps keep the nipple from peeking through.

- **Plunge and push-up** bras are for one thing: to support a low and revealing neckline and to maximize cleavage. The plunge bra tends to be more revealing but with less push-up power. These bras often come with a front clasp, which many women find easier to use.

- **Seamless** bras are what a woman wants for smooth invisible support. A bra should not be part of the visual outfit, and a seamless bra can help make you look great without showing itself off.

+ **Convertible** bras are terrific tools that every woman should have in her wardrobe. The straps are removable and adjustable so that they work for a number of necklines, from racer backs to strapless.

Know what you need your bras to do for you. Keep proper fit and support in mind first. Also consider the material, cut and color. A lace bra will "bleed" through a knit shirt, rather than creating a smooth surface. An unusual neckline, such as a halter top, may require a special bra that will stay neatly concealed underneath the lines of the shirt. A light-colored top needs to be worn with a light bra under it. The best color for maximum discreetness is a flesh colored bra. A nude bra with a smooth finish is invisible under almost anything. It is even more inconspicuous than white, which can show through garments made of thin material. Remember, your bra is supposed to make your clothes look their best. How pretty it is, is not as important as how supportive, smooth, and comfortable it is. Do not let your bras outshine you or your fabulous wardrobe.

The Underestimated Panty

Panties seem like a simple topic, but the truth of the matter is, women should know as much about these little garment necessities as they do about their bras. A great pair of underwear can support you, reduce that unwanted jiggle factor and still feel like they are not even there. A bad pair of underwear can creep up and expose themselves above the waistband or squeeze at your skin and ruin the line of a beautiful pant or skirt. In other words, the wrong choice of underwear can create the worst of offending bulges.

There are four basic panty styles: the brief, the boy brief, the bikini, and the thong. But each one of these styles can vary greatly depending on brand, rise, and material.

Many of my clients have claimed the simple answer to panty line is the thong. While this is true, it really is too simple an answer. There are many styles, cuts and fits of the thong. Everyone finds some types more comfortable than others. The wrong thong on the wrong body can create lines and bulges in all sorts of other unflattering places around the hips and tummy. The thong is also the culprit of the other major panty "faux-pas," the little "Y" that rides up above the waistline at the rear of a low-rise jean. This is not a cute look, no matter how many teenage girls are sporting it! The thong, while often a great solution and surprisingly comfortable at times, is not always the answer.

Another great solution to the panty line that many women ignore is control top panty hose. You can reinforce them with panty liners for moisture, so that underpants are unnecessary. For comfort and breathability cut them off at the knee. This home fix makes the pantyhose much more user-friendly, plus for those of us with some curve or unwanted jiggle in our thigh area; it adds support past the panty area. This is a more binding solution than the thong, but it really does smooth you out for a very chic, well put-together look.

The brief, which basically implies that it has full coverage of the seat, should also not be disregarded. Though the "granny panty" is part of the brief family, it can be a surprisingly flattering panty to smooth you out and avoid ugly lines. These will cover your rear well. The seam should hit right where your leg and your rear meet, so there won't be a line in sight. Now you certainly would not want to wear a high-waisted brief with low-rise jeans, but that is what a low-rise brief is for.

Boy briefs are a cute, newer trend in undies. While not always the best style for hiding lines with a tighter pant, they are a great idea under shorter skirts, and dresses. Boy briefs will help give a more modest girl a little coverage.

It is really important to choose your underwear based on the piece of clothing that will be worn over it. You must consider not only where the seat outline lies against your rear, but also where they hit you at the hips and abdomen.

The other very important element to consider is the material used. Look for tissue thin cotton, nylon, or microfiber bottoms. Generally, I'd advise to steer away from lacey panties for practical use under an outfit, but now in fact there are some wonderfully comfortable brands made of stretchy, soft, lacey material that are not only comfortable, but do not create unwanted lines, bulges or even bleeding. There are also some great seamless styles out there that are made of soft, body-hugging material, rather than body-cutting elastic, so there are barely any noticeable lines.

Try on different brands and new styles. Feel the materials for comfort and the shape for invisibility. You may be surprised!

Shape Wear: The Invisible Image Enhancer

Shape wear is the secret weapon that every woman should have in her closet. No matter how many hours we spend at the gym, and how many diets we follow, time and gravity will eventually catch up with all of our body parts. A great foundation wardrobe is our best defense against time and gravity. I'll tell you a secret: most of the celebrities looking perfect walking down the red carpet are all wearing foundation pieces and shape wear under those gorgeous designer gowns.

Shape wear will help create smoother lines so that your clothes fit and fall around your body just the way they are supposed to. With supportive pieces, you will feel sexy and more confident in your clothes. There is shape wear for nearly every part of your body made of breathable, comfortable materials so that you don't have to feel like you are strapped into an old-fashioned corset or girdle anymore.

There are shapers for nearly every body part. There are waist nippers for an hourglass shape, and Capri's for the entire lower body from the waist down. For those who swear by the thong there are shaper thongs to control the waist and tummy with no panty line! There also are control camisoles for the torso. Control briefs and control slips are all designed to help create control under specific types of bottoms. There is also the body brief, which is a high-waisted boy brief to control the tummy, the derriere, and the upper thigh!

To create your perfect shape wear wardrobe, you must also understand what level of control you desire:

+ **Light control** is usually found in hosiery. It smoothes you out, but does not change your shape.

+ **Medium control** smoothes you out with some compression for a more toned look.

+ **Firm control** gives you maximum compression, which helps you actually appear smaller in clothes.

+ **Extra firm control** is harder to find and usually has added support like boning.

There are a number of different brands of great shape wear. They all have particular aspects or styles that are unique or innovative. It all depends on your particular needs. Again, the feel of the material is usually what motivates a woman to want to wear one of these pieces. Comfort matters; make sure that you are reasonably comfortable with your shape wear. Also keep seam placement in mind. Know where the seams on the pieces are; these can create a whole separate set of unwanted lines. Try the pieces on and make sure the hem of the piece where your body is no longer compressed by the garment is not creating a new bulge. Again, the word "seamless" can be very helpful.

Final Words on Foundations

The quality of the pieces you select will affect how long they last and how well they support you. When the elastic starts to give in any of your undergarments, or they began to lose shape, it is time to say goodbye and do some underwear shopping! Good quality really does make a difference. Your foundation pieces will last longer if you take care of them. It is wise to invest in better brands and take care of them properly so they last a long time. In general, follow the tag instructions for proper care. Some tips, however, are to purchase a mesh bag to wash your bras in and hook the hooks before throwing anything in the wash. You don't have to wash everything after every use. The less you wash them the longer they last, but make sure you let everything properly air out!

In the hotter months I've noticed that women often ignore the need for foundation garments in favor of flimsy materials with no support. When the clothes become less substantial the need for proper support is that much more crucial. Don't forget about your foundation just because more skin is showing. One of the simplest alternatives to shape wear for the upper body is a tank top with a built in bra. Also consider something like control briefs under skirts in the summer months to prevent chafing. A simple summer dress is lovely and will look its best on you if it's supported properly.

In short, nothing works well without a good foundation. There are many factors to consider when creating the right foundation for an outfit. Fit, of course, is your first concern. Cut and texture must be considered for invisibility, so that only you and the outfit are seen. Color must be considered, especially if your outfit has some sheerness to it.

Your perfect wardrobe, with its beautiful pieces, will only look as good as the body underneath. When your body is properly supported with the right undergarments, then the clothes you wear over them will make you look your best.

Know how to buy the right, comfortable, well-fitting underwear for you and your clothes. A stylish girl is prepared for any wardrobe misfit, so create a wardrobe of foundation pieces. You should have a solution for all fit errors so that you always look great and feel confident in all your favorite outfits.

BIANCA STARK-FALCONE, AICI FLC
Well Dressed,
a wardrobe consulting company

You are always at your best when you're well dressed.

(415) 302-5659
lbstarkfalcone@hotmail.com
www.bwelldressed.com

Bianca Stark-Falcone has a flair for fashion and knows how to put it all together. Her undergraduate studies in visual arts and her work within the fashion industry prepared her well for her career as a certified image consultant.

Based in the San Francisco Bay Area, Bianca specializes in wardrobe consultation and personal shopping, ultimately helping her clients build a complete wardrobe, from undergarments to accessories that they can confidently use. Her innate sense of style and sophisticated understanding of how to use clothing to best flatter the human body has allowed Bianca to build a cadre of satisfied clients. Bianca's goal is to build a stylish wardrobe that projects confidence and personality and works for all aspects of her client's lifestyle.

Creating a Winning Wardrobe

Essentials That Ensure You Always Look Your Best

By Rosa Maria Livesay, AICI FLC

Every day, when a woman gets dressed, she faces the challenge of what to wear and how to put together an outfit that will make her look her best. It doesn't matter if you're a stay-at-home mom, CEO of a company, a student or an up-and-coming entrepreneur. We all face the same dilemma, but never fear: the solution is at your fingertips. In this chapter you'll discover the simple steps every woman needs to follow to create a winning wardrobe.

Contrary to the fashion forecasters, the current styles and fashions may not be for everyone. By creating a basic winning wardrobe, you will no longer face the challenge of having a closet full of clothes and feeling like you have nothing to wear. Plus, you can update your wardrobe with just a new piece or two, or by adding accessories to give you a fresh new look without compromising your style or spending a fortune. When you build a winning wardrobe, you will always have a fabulous look, and a perfect outfit to wear each and every time.

There are some important elements to consider before learning how you can create your basic winning wardrobe with just a few essentials.

Only Select Pieces That Fit and Flatter Your Shape and Body

Do not be persuaded by the allure and glamour of the runway shows or fashion magazines, or the many makeover shows that have sprung up. The currents styles may not be *your* style. Choose styles that are right for you before investing your money.

When you're not 100 percent sure which styles work for you, consider investing in the services of an image consultant. She can help educate you about styles that will make you look fabulous and give the illusion of having a perfectly proportioned body. Hiring a consultant is not a luxury. It is an essential. You will find that shopping will become a breeze. Shopping with more confidence will save you money and give you a closet full of wonderful things to wear to help you look your best.

Choose Colors that Complement Your Hair, Skin Tone, and Eye Color

Every spring and fall, fashion magazines and designer runway shows lure you into believing that the new color palettes are right for you. Designers and makeover shows make it very tempting to purchase the current season's colors. Don't fall into this trap and add the wrong colors to your wardrobe.

You can still add an occasional color you've never worn but make sure it's a color that is right for you. There will be seasons when there is nothing in your colors. This is great because you will not be tempted to spend a lot. Remember next season the stores might be flooded with what's right for you. Think of the shopping spree you will have with the money you saved from the previous season. The new color palette just might fill your closet.

If you are not color savvy, and even if you think you might know your correct colors, I recommend you hire a color expert. It will make a world of difference and you'll be amazed at the array of colors that can enhance your look.

Once you have learned what styles and colors work best for you, you can then begin to create your personalized wardrobe that includes the essentials you need to always look your best. I use the term *essential*, also known as a "core wardrobe." These essentials create confidence and control. By mixing and matching essential pieces you will have numerous new outfits.

Six Elements of a Winning Essential Wardrobe

As you begin to build an essential wardrobe, there are certain elements you have to remember. These six elements along with the right style and color will give you the perfect outfit each and every time.

1. **Consider your essential wardrobe pieces as investments.** Select quality over price every time. This will ensure that your essential wardrobe pieces will last for years to come. When you're on a budget you may have to build your essential wardrobe over time. Here is a simple solution: pick one must-have piece and save for it. Adding a piece at a time takes the hassle out of trying to purchase an entire wardrobe all at once, and is easier on your budget.

2. **Select fabrics that are durable and ageless.** For example, if you choose an ensemble made up of a jacket, skirt, and

pants, wool or wool blends like a wool gabardine or wool crepe are ideal fabric choices. They are cool in summer and warm in winter. Choose fabrics that are durable and don't have to be replaced every season.

3. **Select styles that are timeless.** If you are trying to create a new wardrobe, or adding to your wardrobe, choose styles that will always be right for you. They can be updated combining them with a new piece or by adding accessories that are trendy.

4. **Make sure any new pieces work with what you already have.** When selecting individual pieces, in lieu of an ensemble, they must look like they belong together. It's not just color —you have to make sure that the fabric textures work well with each other. Some fabrics are not compatible.

5. **Wear the right foundation garments.** A good foundation is extremely important. It's truly essential to get your clothing to look and fit like a million dollars. Foundations can make or break an outfit. See Bianca Stark-Falcone's chapter, "Foundation Pieces: The Secret Behind Every Beautiful Curve."

6. **Think versatility.** As you start to select essential pieces for your wardrobe, think versatility. Versatility gives you the freedom to dress up your wardrobe for that business or formal look, or dress down for the business casual or casual look. You want to have a wardrobe full of pieces you can dress up for that business meeting, and then dress down for an afternoon out with your friends.

Essentials to Always Look Your Best

There are certain essentials every woman must have in her closet. Whether you're a stay-at-home mom who finds T-shirts and jeans the best attire to keep up with young toddlers, or an executive who wears professional attire every day, certain things apply to every woman.

The essential items for your wardrobe are grouped together into five sections. Each section describes the use of the items or garments and how you can work them into your wardrobe.

Dress Up and Dress Down Essentials

This first group is made up of the essentials you will be able to dress up or down, use for the office, for a dinner out or for a special occasion.

+ **A dress.** Add the "little black dress" to your closet. If black is not in your color palette, then add the darkest shade that looks great on you. This way you will always have something to wear. Unless an invitation or event specifies "black attire" your darkest shade will work. It is appropriate as a cocktail dress or for a semi-formal occasion. For party events, add a little glitter or some glitzy accessories and you are set. You can pick a sleeveless sheath dress out of a silk blend crepe, or a light weight gabardine. With it you can wear a buttoned jacket in the same color and fabric. This is a cool summer look and very chic for those special events in the summer or any warm weather climate.

+ **A tailored suit.** A suit is a very versatile item for your wardrobe, especially if you can find a three-piece suit made up of a jacket, skirt, and pants. Remember, in order for it to look like a million dollars, you need to get a style that is right for you. Choose your suit in one of your darker colors so that when you wear it, it will give you a very professional look, with an air of strength and confidence. Wear your jacket especially when you want to be taken seriously; it is a sure sign of authority. Jackets are not only worn over skirts and pants, but can be worn over a dress giving you a variety of outfits. Some women choose to select individual pieces in lieu of an ensemble. This can be done if they look like they belong together, so pay close attention to color, fabric, texture, and style.

Essential Tops

The second group of essential items is made up of pieces that you can wear with your jacket, skirt, or pants.

+ **A shell**. This is a top that can have sleeves or be sleeveless. It has no collar and can be made out of a knit or a natural fiber. To dress up an outfit, chose a shell made out of silk. Shells are great because they don't wrinkle and always look good.

+ **A sweater.** The sweater can be a cardigan, or a long cowl-neck tunic, or a twin sweater set (sweater with matching shell) which gives you more versatility. A soft cardigan sweater made of a silk-cashmere knit is so comfortable and luxurious to wear. Or get a long cowl-neck sweater made of a soft cotton jersey, and wear it with a long dark skirt out of the same material. This is a phenomenal look. There are also turtlenecks or mock turtleneck sweaters. The turtleneck has a close-fitting high collar that folds over and covers the neck. The mock turtleneck is a collar that stands up around your neck. This style is fantastic if you have a shorter neck.

Inside and Outside Essentials

This third group is made up of essential items than can be worn inside or outside of the above garments. They can be a main essential or can be used as decoration.

- ♦ **A scarf.** Scarves are very versatile items. They can be worn over your shoulder or around your neck. They can also be worn over your head. You can put them inside your coat or jacket to keep you warm, or simply wear one outside of those outer garments as a decorative piece. Scarves made out of silk or made by a designer such as Hermès®, Gucci® or Yves St. Laurent®, to name a few, will add elegance to any outfit. To keep you warm try a scarf made of silk wool or cashmere, and if you are on a budget a soft knit scarf will work too. Scarves come in all shapes and sizes. If you have trouble figuring out how to wear them, try taking an accessories workshop. You can also work with your image consultant to help find the best use of scarves for you.

- ♦ **A shawl.** This is a great addition to any wardrobe. It can be worn around your shoulders to keep you warm, or over your shoulder as a decorative accessory. Unlike scarves, shawls are large pieces of fabric, usually cut in a square and may have fringe. Depending on the fabric, they can help dress down or dress up an outfit.

- ♦ **A coat.** No matter where you live, you will find that a coat is an essential item. A wool gabardine coat is great for cold climates or for an evening out. Depending on your style, a duster coat is great for milder weather. Some consider a trench coat the prime essential piece, instead of a regular coat, because it's a raincoat. It is usually waterproof and often has a removable insulated lining for colder weather. In mild weather you can remove the liner, giving you more versatility. They can be made of wool, cotton twill, leather, and even satin for evening. The fabric of your trench coat will be determined by the climate you live in. Try to stay away from synthetic fabrics because they don't breathe. They usually retain perspiration odors, and can be hard to clean once soiled.

Accessory Essentials

The fourth group is made up of those accessories that can make or break an outfit.

- **A few good quality pairs of leather shoes.** Consider a flat, a low-to-moderate heel, and pair of high heels for the evening. Good quality leather is a must, because it's easy to maintain and will last a long time. Make sure you find a reliable, competent cobbler to maintain the look of your shoes. Here quality reigns over price.

- **A pair of leather boots.** Boots are a great essential for your wardrobe. Like shoes they should be made of good quality leather. They can be worn under skirts, dresses, or pants. The choices are unlimited. Boots come with flat and low-to-moderate heels, as well as high heels. They can be short ankle height or as high as your thigh.

- **A quality leather handbag and belt.** Leather will set you apart from the ordinary. It is durable and can take you from day into evening. Select belts and handbags with classic styling that will work with your other essential wardrobe components.

Those Essential Extras

This last group includes what I call extra essentials. Add them as you can for more style and versatility.

- **A great pair of jeans.** They are a great essential that you can dress up or dress down easily. When adding a great pair of jeans you might prefer a designer style or a designer who makes jeans for your type of figure. The fit will make or break the jeans, so find a good tailor or seamstress who can alter your jeans for the perfect fit.

- **A tailored shirt.** This essential will look great under a jacket, over a skirt, pants or pair of jeans. This is considered a "must have" item in your closet. Chose a shirt in white or a light color. If pure white is not in your color palette, make sure you get a shirt in *your* white. Brooks Brothers® makes the ultimate tailored shirt for women. It is a "women's non-iron miracle shirt" that is fitted, washable and always looks like new.

- **A pair of tailored pants.** Make sure that you purchase them in a dark solid color, and good quality; they will be worth the expense. You can add softer or lighter shades of colors in your tops, sweaters, and accessories. Like everything else, make sure that the fit and style are perfect for you. They should also be comfortable and easy to dress up or down.

- **A skirt.** Choose a style that is just right for you and that fits perfectly. The principles for tailored pants apply to skirts as well. Find the best style for you. A great skirt will make an excellent addition to your wardrobe.

Now You Have the Essentials for a Winning Wardrobe

When you have these fundamental items in your wardrobe you will always have the perfect outfit to wear and always look fabulous.

After reading this chapter you might feel like you want to go shopping right away. Don't. Go to your closet first. How many of the essential wardrobe pieces do you already have that you have overlooked? Once you know what is in your closet, then go shopping to fill in the blanks. Most important, have fun and know that with these winning wardrobe essentials you will always look your very best.

ROSA MARIA LIVESAY, AICI FLC
RML Images

Always be the best YOU!

(408) 254-3203
rml@rmlimages.com
www.rmlimages.com

Since 1993 Rosa Maria has worked with men and women of all ages to help them be the best they can be by helping them enhance their image. She guides her clients through the maze of clothing shapes, styles, and color choices. Her forte is showing her clients how to build the right wardrobe that suits their personality and lifestyle. She helps her clients identify good quality and value when shopping and ultimately saves them time and money.

Always passionate about color, Rosa Maria has studied the subject extensively and considers it one of her key areas of expertise. When working with individuals she makes sure they're dressing for success and includes business etiquette and communication skills training. She strives to help her clients achieve an effortless and natural look that is timeless and enhances their style.

Rosa Maria is currently the President of the San Francisco Bay Area Chapter of AICI (Association of Image Consultants International). She is a certified consultant of AICI and CTI—(Crowning Touch Institute) and Universal Style International (Consultant for Women). She is an associate member of CDI—(Colour Designers International) and FGI—(Fashion Group International). Rosa Maria offers workshops in both Spanish and English.

Get Out of Your Closet in Seven Minutes—Looking Great!

How Being Disorganized Can Ruin Your Appearance

By Leah Oman, AICI CIP

"O-o-o-o-o-oh, you *really* wouldn't want to look in *my* closet!" That's what I often hear when I'm telling a woman about my services and get to the part about closet assessments. I assure her that I'm not easily shocked by *closet chaos*. I've seen plenty of it. In fact, her closet couldn't possibly be any worse than mine when I was in my twenties and thirties.

What about you? Is your closet jam-packed and messy? Do you have trouble finding what you were hoping to wear? Imagine this scenario: You try on a dozen garments, don't like what you see in the mirror and take them off again. Time is flying by, and you're still not dressed. You know you're going to skip breakfast, get caught in the worst traffic, and be totally stressed-out by the time you get to work. You finally give up and put on whatever you grab next. Then, you feel uncomfortable in it all day because it's a little tighter than you remember, or the color makes you look ill, or the hem is coming out. Sound familiar? Then this information is for you!

You may have lived in dread of your closet for years, but catching on to the following strategies and taking action on them will render your closet space more user-friendly (and your life easier). As a recovering closet chaos avoider, I'd like to share them with you, so you can get in and out of your closet in minutes, looking great—and feeling confident and relaxed.

Your Closet Doesn't Have to Be a Jungle Adventure

Imagine a boat trip into the deepest jungles of the Amazon. Natives on the riverbank; poison dart guns pointed straight at you; a python slithering across the tree branch overhead. Danger, the unknown, mosquitoes! You never know what you'll run into next. It can be downright terrifying!

Could you stand the anxiety—the dread—the hassle of that *every* day? Well, you may be experiencing it already if whenever you enter your closet, it's a "jungle" in there and you ask yourself, "What am I going to put on this morning that looks the *least* awful? Is there anything without wrinkles or spots or split seams? What do I own that will make a good impression on that new client? Yikes, I don't have anything to wear!"

It doesn't have to be that way. Imagine how freeing it would be to walk out your front door in the morning knowing that you look great—and ready to make a positive impression on everyone you meet.

Dealing with the jungle can feel overwhelming. But, believe me, even a disorganized person can have an organized closet: a stress-free corner you can feel good about every morning. I should know. I've been to the jungle and came back alive. Here's how to do it.

Hacking Your Way Through the Jungle

Don't even consider tackling the entire closet in one go. Your closet didn't disintegrate overnight, and you don't have to rebuild it in a day. Think in terms of small steps. Doing a *small something* is better than doing a *big nothing*. With a few simple tactics, you can get that unruly growth under control.

Begin by removing anything that you're not wearing right now because:

- **It doesn't fit anymore.** You may want to save it until you lose that 10 pounds you gained over the holidays, but at least get it out of your closet and out of sight, so it doesn't seem like a choice when it really isn't.

- **It's not in season.** If so, it's better not to mix it in with your workable wardrobe. Store it. If you don't have an extra closet, you can buy a portable wardrobe container or a rolling rack that can be covered. Scrambling through heavy woolens in the summer or sheer linens in the winter is distracting when you're rushing to get dressed.

- **You haven't worn it for a year or more.** It may be a good candidate for donation or resale at a consignment shop. If you don't remember if you've worn it in the past year, here's a tip: Hang every garment facing the same direction. After you've worn something, turn it to face the opposite direction. After a year, you should be suspicious of anything not facing the opposite direction. You can then decide if you want to take it out of the lineup and release it, or continue to hold it captive. However, ask yourself why you haven't worn it for that long. If it's a special occasion piece that you rarely wear, could you find another storage place for it?

+ **You feel guilty about getting rid of it.** Did you spend a whole month's paycheck on it, but it was never quite right? Is it a gift from your Aunt Hilda—and you wouldn't wear it if your house was on fire and it was the only thing hanging in your closet? Do you have trouble getting rid of anything because you "might need it someday?" Guilt reasons are dead weight that can hold you down. By moving the garment along *now*, and not seeing it anymore, your guilt can be over quickly, reducing your stress quotient.

+ **It never really suited you in the first place.** Maybe you didn't realize until a few months after you bought it that the color walks in the door before you do, or the style doesn't flatter your body type, or that print makes you look like a fairy princess when you really prefer more of a sporty style. Consider it an expensive lesson, one you won't repeat.

+ **It's out-of-date.** It should be out the door. If it has sentimental value, pack it away.

+ **It's rumpled, stained, needing repair, or otherwise not wearable.** Put it aside—possibly into a large bag that you keep in your car trunk so you can drop it off when you pass by your cleaners, shoe repair or tailor.

+ **It's an orphan.** This item doesn't go with anything else in your closet. You'll need to determine if it's worth spending more money to find it a couple of friends, or better to let it go. One quick way to know if it's a keeper is to wear it out somewhere this week and notice how you feel in it. If you feel good, hang it back in your closet. If you don't feel good, that's a strong sign that you won't be wearing it much in the future, and it's probably time to move it along.

There now! You've wielded your machete and cleared a path in your closet. By this time it should be a lot easier to get dressed because you'll only have the garments you actually wear hanging there. Isn't it an awesome feeling to have the debris cleared away? Take a deep breath. You deserve a break!

After removing what's not working from your closet, you may still notice you can't *always* find what you need right away. You think there might be more to this process. And, you'd be right! That's why we're moving on from the jungle cruise to the next step: getting everything into its rightful place.

Why Can't I Find It When I Need It?

Cooking schools were all the rage in the late 1970s. Since I was living in Europe at the time, I signed up for some classes in Paris. One Saturday morning, Master Pastry Chef Albert demonstrated how to make a pear tart. The aroma in the kitchen was tantalizing. When his assistant took it warm from the oven, my mouth was watering. They sliced it up and handed it out for tasting. Fork poised, I dug in.

I was all set to savor the sweet pastry, the creamy filling, the melt-in-your-mouth pears. But, on first bite, I noticed something strange. The tart seemed to be sucking up all the saliva in my mouth. Disbelieving, I tried a second bite. In a couple of seconds, I spit it back out on the plate. It tasted like The Great Salt Lake. One of Chef Albert's assistants had accidentally filled up the sugar container with salt. The tart had been prepared with a *cup* of salt and a *pinch* of sugar.

A sign hung on the kitchen wall of that Parisian Cooking School saying in French, "A place for everything and everything in its place." Chef Albert's demo instantly proved the wisdom of that saying. Finding a place for everything, and putting it there, seems easier said than done for those of us born without the organizational gene. But it *can* be done more easily than you might think. You just need a strategy to break down the process into manageable parts. Here are some tips to help you get started:

- **First,** hang all like garments together—suits, jackets, shirts, knit tops, pants, and dresses should each be separated into their own sections.

- **Second,** arrange each section according to color—all the blue items together, all the reds, greens, blacks, etc. It'll be easier to scan the contents of your closet and find what you're looking for.

- **Third,** get all your shoes on racks or into clear plastic boxes. Leaving them in a jumble on the closet floor and stumbling over them adds to your frustration when you're pushed for time.

- **Fourth,** fold your sweaters and delicate knits and stack them on shelves (again in clear plastic boxes) if you have the space, or get an enclosed, see-through container of hanging shelves. If your space is limited, you may need to tuck them away into drawers, but being able to see them helps you remember to wear them.

- **Lastly,** find ways to hang all your accessories, too, if possible. Specialized hangers exist for just about everything, including scarves, belts, and necklaces. There are even plastic pocketed hanging containers for earrings and bracelets. Hang your necklaces carefully with space between them to avoid the agony of untangling a knotted necklace when you're in a hurry.

Keeping everything readily visible helps you remember what you have to wear. That way, instead of finding it in some dark corner collecting dust-balls five years after it's gone out of style, you can actually put it on *now* and feel good about it.

At this point, you can find everything you need when you need it. What a relief! But there's still one more step to getting out the door looking great. Whatever you put on has to be in good condition and ready to go.

How to Avoid Wardrobe Breakdown

Three months after we got married, my husband Bob and I bought a used VW bug to chug around Europe. Our car engine blew up somewhere between Amsterdam and Copenhagen. Bob didn't believe in car maintenance. He avoided filling the gas tank until the gauge read slightly below empty.

When we finally rolled into a service station for lack of fuel, the attendant asked if we also wanted to have the "oily" checked. Bob cheerfully, but firmly, said "No, thanks," and I deferred to my new husband, and let it go. Less than an hour later, we were both sorry. The car broke down because there wasn't any "oily" in the engine.

Wardrobes are like cars. They malfunction without maintenance. Both need to be kept in good condition if they're going to function well—or at all. Are your shoes looking a bit scruffy? Has a button fallen off your jacket? Is a stain on your shirt talking louder than you? Does everything in your closet feel too tight or too loose?

There is a simpler way to live:

♦ **First of all,** buy clothes that are wash and wear. Otherwise, recognize that you need to pay for dry cleaning. If you're really pressed for time, send your laundry to the cleaners too. And you may need two dry cleaners: one that's cheap for most of your clothes and one that's more expensive if you're worried that your most treasured dress could come back resembling Cinderella's rags.

- **Second,** when a button goes missing, a seam comes undone, or you find evidence of last night's dinner on your shirt, put the garment either in a large bag to be kept in the trunk of your car or in a reserved section at the back of the closet with a paper note poked onto the hanger to remind you what needs to be done to it. Then, remember to get it fixed within the month or two, at the most. By the way, a really good service-oriented dry cleaner usually does minor repairs too. You may have to search for one, but they do exist so don't settle for less!

- **Third,** a couple of times a year take your scuffed up shoes in for cleaning and polishing. Have those worn-down heels replaced. And try not to wear the same pair day after day. They need a breather if you want them to last. Also, find a cobbler who can repair handbags or shorten belts when you lose weight.

- **Fourth,** if you lose weight, take your "too big" clothing to the tailor and have it altered. If you gain weight, get your "too small" clothing out of the closet and store it somewhere else until you can fit in it again. Either way, poor fit drags down your appearance and your image. Getting the right fit increases your credibility.

- **Finally,** keep all your other accessories in good shape. Repair broken jewelry. Worn looking belts or bags or frayed edges on anything will scream that you're less than attentive to detail—an instant image breaker.

Consistent maintenance makes your wardrobe last longer and polishes your appearance. Just as your car needs a good mechanic, your shoes, clothes, and accessories need professional service too.

Your wardrobe is a resource for making you competitive in the workplace, confident at social events, and happier with yourself. Organization and maintenance are the keys for getting in and out of your closet quickly. These are not glamorous or sexy words, but consider the advantages:

You're more relaxed about getting dressed which shows up in your face and your entire appearance. You're more in control of your life, which makes you feel calmer, stronger and more confident. You're put-together and ready to impress everyone by your competent demeanor, which allows you to stop worrying about how you look. That way you can focus on the things that matter most to you, such as your career or relationships.

To sum up, three simple steps will get you to a stress-free closet:

- **First,** remove everything from your closet that you're not currently wearing.
- **Second,** organize everything that's remaining.
- **Third,** keep the contents of your closet in good condition.

What's next for you?

Are you going to settle for the anxiety, dread, and hassle of your messy, disorganized closet every morning? Or would you prefer to saunter into your closet, effortlessly choose something to wear, and emerge in minutes—feeling calm, confident, attractive, and ready to cruise through your day? That's what I thought.

LEAH OMAN, MA, AICI CIP
The Smarter Image, Inc.

(303) 471-733
leah@thesmarterimage.com
www.thesmarterimage.com

Based in Denver, Colorado, Leah Oman is an AICI Certified Image Professional and CEO of The Smarter Image, Inc., a company created to help business and professional women optimize their appearance and increase their confidence. Leah understands the frustration of women who would rather scrub floors than shop for clothes—and she's delighted to hear her clients say, "That's the first time I've ever had fun shopping!"

Working with women in transition is Leah's specialty. Whether you're starting a new career, a new lifestyle, or a new relationship, she brings together the look that feels right for you. You won't have an image imposed on you. You won't have to change who you are. You'll still be *you*—feeling fabulous about the way you look. Leah provides closet therapy as well as personal shopping services. She shows you how to pump up your image power by helping you create a wardrobe that really works for you—personally and professionally.

As a trainer and consultant, Leah has worked with major corporations and educational institutions in Asia, Europe and the U.S. She speaks regularly on the power of image, how to dress effectively, and the importance of color "communication." When she's not dressing women in the greater Denver area, Leah enjoys scuba diving, world travel and shopping around the globe.

Shop Like a Pro and Look Like a Million Bucks!

A Guide to Saving Time, Money and Reducing Stress

By Dana Lynch, AICI FLC

Even though every man I speak with is convinced that all women love to shop, I know that is not the truth. The vast majority of my clients dislike shopping. There are many reasons women prefer not to shop, but the one that I hear most often is that shopping is exhausting and overwhelming.

I have always loved shopping, but even a professional shopper like me has made mistakes in the past. Some of my real flubs taught me valuable lessons for improving my shopping techniques. The following tips can help you turn what you might consider a distasteful task into a tolerable, and possibly even an enjoyable one. If you already enjoy shopping, you'll find these guidelines can help you save money, be more efficient, and you'll come home from your shopping trips more fulfilled than ever.

Set a Goal for Every Shopping Trip

We set goals for other areas of our lives: our finances, education, retirement, and even less important things like travel. Why wouldn't we set goals for shopping and building our wardrobes when we know how important our image is to our success in so many areas of our lives? So what kinds of goals might you have for shopping? Perhaps you simply need a few accessories to finish a few outfits. Perhaps an entire season's wardrobe is on the bill, or maybe your goal is as simple as wanting a new outfit to pick up your spirits.

No matter how big or small your goal, planning and setting goals for your shopping trips will not only help alleviate some of the stress you may associate with shopping, you'll also know when you've achieved your goals. This gives you a feeling of success, not to mention a better wardrobe and image!

The following four steps are essential to planning a successful shopping trip and a well-planned wardrobe:

1. **Get clear on your personal style.**
   In its simplest sense, discovering your personal style is taking the time to decide which lines, shapes, colors, textures, and patterns you like, and the ones you don't like. Then the key is staying true to it. For example, if orange happens to be the hot color of the season and you can't stand it or the way it looks on you, feel free to skip it! Your favorite color may be the hot color next season. Once you've found your personal style, it's still important to keep abreast of what's current, but knowing your style can save you from a lot of "fashion mistakes" in your closet. Knowing your personal style allows you to stay focused when shopping, saving both time and money!

2. **Take inventory of your closet to identify any gaps.**

   Taking inventory of your clothing may first require a little organization—so that you can see exactly what you've got. I recommend doing this exercise when you've finished the laundry and picked up the dry cleaning. Really analyze what you have and how it's working for you.

   Consider what new pieces would serve you best. For example, if you have several suits with an equal number of blouses, you will most likely need more tops. Or if you have mostly skirts, and you have recently decided you're tired of wearing heels all of the time, you'd be wise to invest in some well-made slacks.

3. **Identify your lifestyle needs.**

   Take a few minutes to think about what activities you spend most of your time doing. Whatever type of clothing you need to be most successful in those activities is where you want to be putting most of your clothing dollars. As an image consultant, I work primarily with busy, success-oriented professional women. Because there are so many outdoor activities here in Colorado, I find that many of my clients have far more fleece jackets than professional jackets in their closets. There's nothing wrong with this; it's actually pretty natural. However, if you work in an office environment, having enough variety in your professional clothing will not only make you appear more successful, but you'll also feel less stressed when you're getting dressed!

4. **Make a shopping list.**

   Once you've evaluated your likes and dislikes, inventoried your wardrobe, and identified your lifestyle needs, it's time to make your shopping list. A list is especially helpful if you need something specific, like a wide brown belt to update a few outfits, or the perfect pair of shoes to go with your interview suit. In addition to your list, if you've found clothes and accessories you love in magazines, tear those pages out and take them with you. Showing your pictures to a salesperson can be a major time saver.

Even if you can visualize exactly what you need, writing it down will help you stay focused while you're shopping. Even though you may not always know *exactly* what you're looking for when you go shopping, the simple act of writing down notes and ideas of what you want can help bring it into view for you. And if you don't find everything that's on your list on your first trip out, you can keep it in your purse and when you find you've got some extra time to pop into a store, your list is right there.

Although there's nothing wrong with being a little spontaneous, having a plan when you go shopping allows you to focus and be productive at what can sometimes be a confusing, overwhelming and daunting task!

Buy Complete Outfits

When you find something, whether at full price or on sale, either build a complete outfit around it or make certain you've got something at home that will match. You may think "I'll find something to wear with it later," or "Surely I can wear it with a white top," but chances are good you'll put it in your closet, with tags still attached, and forget about it. When you finally realize you've never worn the piece, it will most likely be too late to take it back.

I've worked with hundreds of clients and their closets. You can take comfort in knowing that almost everyone has clothes in their closets that have been there for a long time, with tags still on them. And most of the time it's because there's nothing else in the closet that the items remotely match. More often than not the client is ambivalent about the item, and it ends up in the giveaway pile. I'm certainly not judging anyone, but every time this happens I feel a twinge of pain and visualize money going right into the shredder. Think of all of the shoes you could have bought.

Only Buy Clothes You Absolutely Love

Although I highly recommend experimenting and trying on clothes you may not love at first, I am *adamant* that you must love what you take home. I really see this as a sign of self-respect. What you wear is a big part of who you are. If you want to feel fabulous and look like a million bucks, why would you settle? There are countless brands and styles out there, and I truly believe there's something perfect out there for everyone. Buying clothes that are just "okay" leads to a closet full of clothes that you're dissatisfied with and won't wear.

There is one caveat here: the basics. Basics are exactly what they sound like—pieces that are relatively plain and without much detail. There may not be much to love about a pair of simple black or khaki pants or a plain white blouse. What you should love though, is how the garment fits and flatters your body, and of course, it should be comfortable.

Don't Be Seduced by the Price

Another point to keep in mind is to make sure you really love the item, not just the price. Many women I know, myself included, love to find a bargain. When you're shopping end-of-season sales and outlet stores, stop and ask yourself, "Would I buy this at full price?" Of course we all have budgets to follow, but if your answer is "no," chances are good that you're being lured by the price, not the garment. Chances are doubly good that if you fall prey to pricing and don't absolutely love what you buy for its own merits, it will hang in your closet unworn.

On the flip side of this issue, if you're shopping and you find a garment that's a *little* out of your price range, but you've fallen head over heels for it and it makes you look ten pounds thinner, it's the perfect color, and you know it will go with multiple things in your closet, consider buying that garment and foregoing a couple of other things in your "yes" pile. The price may hurt a little, but in the long run you'll find you wear this piece over and over again, a true value.

Lastly, I know that especially if you don't like shopping and you don't have a lot of time to shop, it can be tempting to settle on an item on your shopping list versus going home from a shopping trip empty-handed. Don't do it! It's okay to go home without buying anything! By staying true to yourself and only buying clothes that you love, you'll start to build the wardrobe you've always dreamed about—the one that will make you feel and look as fabulous as you are!

Try Clothes On When You Go Shopping

I know it can be tempting to run into a store and quickly pick something up without trying it on. The problem is that most of us don't have three-way mirrors at home, and we may not scrutinize the fit as well as we would at the store. Check yourself out from all angles in a three-way mirror. You may be surprised. I've tried on lots of great outfits, and then I check the back and think, "Oh, maybe not!"

Often when you take clothes home without trying them on, you will find that they may fit, but they don't look exactly the way you'd imagined, and you're only lukewarm about the garment or outfit. This is yet another way you can end up with a closet full of so-so clothes versus a closet full of clothes you love.

It truly takes a lot less time to try the clothing on the first time you're in the store than to have to get back in your car and take another shopping trip!

You May Have to Try on Many Pairs of Pants to Find a Great Fit

I ask all of my clients what's the hardest garment for them to find, and it's almost always pants. If you think about it, pants have to fit us in a lot of places!

Know that you are not alone. There's nothing wrong with your body! Plan to take some time to try on pants, and take a boatload into the fitting room. It's normal! Keep in mind you may still have to have a couple of alterations done. The confidence you'll gain knowing your clothes fit and look great is well worth the time, effort and price!

Pay Attention to the Quality of Garments

Look at fabrics. Do they drape nicely or are they stiff or even worse, clingy? Check the construction. Are there a lot of loose threads? Check the stitching. Look for small stitches that lie flat without any puckering.

Most of the time, you get what you pay for. Unless, of course, you've just found the bargain of the century! Spending a little more money can provide more wearings per garment—the true test of value. I'm not advocating that you go out and spend a fortune for your clothes. I just simply want you to be aware of quality, and steer clear of items that don't pass the test.

One last word on quality: Lately, several discount stores have been bringing in top designers, and upping their fashion quotient. They've also been increasing their prices. I suggest you do a little "investigative shopping" and check out some stores you may think are out of your price range. Sometimes you'll find these fashionable clothes for just a few dollars more at far better quality. This makes for value!

Shop Alone

I know it sounds lonely, but unless it's a fun girl's day out, and you don't care if you find anything, go by yourself or with your personal shopper! I find that when I am looking for something specific, I'm either distracted by my companions or I feel guilty taking all the time I need to try enough clothes on to find what I'm looking for and what suits me perfectly.

Another thing that can happen when you go shopping with your husband, pal, or relative is that they may not give you objective opinions about what you're trying on. They may try to persuade you to try on clothes that are their personal style, not yours. Or worse, they may limit you and put you in a box. You might hear things like, "Well, I've *never* seen you in anything that bright before!" A comment like this usually comes right after you've determined you love the color and know it looks great on you.

If you're truly uncomfortable making decisions about what looks good and what doesn't, try to find a salesperson and ask her for an honest opinion, letting her know you appreciate her and you'll buy *something,* but it's got to be the right thing. As a last resort, take a friend with you who you know doesn't have expectations of you. Let her know you trust her. Make a deal with her that this trip will be all about you and the next one will be her time.

I know it seems like it would be easier and more fun to shop with friends, but if you have limited time to shop, you'll truly be more productive by yourself.

Dress Nicely When You Go Shopping

When I was much younger and didn't give as much thought to what I was wearing, I always thought salespeople were being snobs for not helping me. What I've learned over the years, and through my image training, is that people are attracted to others who have taken the time to dress appropriately and attractively. Dress nicely and you'll get much better service. I promise!

It's also important to do your hair and make-up as you normally would. It's hard to look in the mirror and imagine how a garment is going to look when you're not wearing make-up and your hair isn't done.

Lastly, try to wear clothes that are easy to remove. Avoid a lot of buttons and lace-up shoes. You won't be motivated to take many trips into the dressing room when you know getting reassembled afterwards is going to be such a hassle!

In a nutshell, dress nice and easy! You'll get better service. You'll get a true vision of how the clothes will flatter you, and you'll be motivated to take enough trips into the dressing room to accomplish all of your shopping goals.

Take Water, Snacks and Take Time for Yourself

Most of my clients deem me tireless. As much as I love to shop, even *I* find it tiring sometimes. I attribute my shopping stamina to a positive attitude and my water. Many times when you think you're tired or hungry, you're just thirsty. If this is your case, drink a little water and you'll be as good as new.

If you are truly hungry, take a break and have a snack or light lunch to keep your energy up while shopping.

Lastly, it's important to take time for yourself when you're shopping. As I mentioned earlier, it can be tempting to run into the mall on your way home from work or on your lunch hour. I've even seen women run into a store, hastily pick out a few items and wear them out of the store to an event. Although shopping doesn't have to be a marathon or become the focal point of your life, it does take some time to:

- View yourself from all angles
- Analyze the fit
- Determine if it's right for your body type
- Put together a complete outfit, including accessories
- Think about how the purchase will fit into your wardrobe as a whole, and most important
- Decide if you absolutely love it

Depending on the length of your shopping list, set aside enough time when you're well rested and relaxed to find the clothes you need and love. And to help ensure a successful trip, don't forget your water and snacks.

Educate Yourself

If you cringed when you read the tip to "shop alone," consider hiring an image consultant to teach you how to shop and what your best choices are. Besides helping you see your assets, an image consultant will teach you how to:

- Camouflage your figure liabilities
- Shop for your personal style and budget
- Spot a true bargain
- Choose clothing that will fit into your wardrobe and lifestyle

Using an image consultant can be a fun way to increase your shopping savvy and learn all the things about shopping your mother never taught you. Not to mention, when you become more confident with your shopping skills and decisions, it just might become one of your favorite activities!

Whether you like shopping or not, following these tips can help make any shopping trip more successful. Saving money or getting a good value is just the icing on the cake. When you stick to your plan, buying only things you love, you'll find shopping is rewarding and you'll be on your way to always looking like a million bucks.

DANA LYNCH, AICI FLC
Elements of Image

Take the stress out of getting dressed!

(303) 463-4839
dana@elementsofimage.com
www.elementsofimage.com

Dana Lynch specializes in professional dress and has worked with attorneys, mortgage brokers, real estate agents, CPAs, financial planners, and countless other professionals. Using the elements of design and the universal factors of non-verbal communications, Dana has proven, time and time again, that one's image can be used to gain an edge in the workplace to help achieve success.

Dana is a sought-after speaker on the topics of professional dress and effective business-casual dressing. Some of her clients include Hensel Phelps Construction, Hitachi Consulting, Encana Gas & Oil USA, the Colorado State Patrol, and the West Denver Chamber of Commerce. Her passionate, approachable speaking style motivates audience members to reflect on their own image and decide if it is helping or hurting them in their careers.

Dana has authored many articles on image and fashion, has been quoted as an expert in the *Wall Street Journal* and was profiled by *Colorado Expression Magazine* as a top Denver, Colorado image consultant. Additionally, she writes a weekly blog, an e-Style Tip of the Month, and is a regular contributor to the *APW Communiqué's* "Dear Dana" column.

Are You Having a Fit About Fit?

How Your Clothes Fit Can Make or Break
Our Overall Image

By Helena Chenn, AICI CIP

Can't find clothes to fit? When you put on a jacket in the stores, are the sleeves always too long or too full? How about pants? Is the waist too tight? Do they always ride up? Are the hems too long or too short? Do you think it is just *your* body that is difficult to fit?

Each year, approximately $28 billion worth of merchandise is returned to stores because of poor fit. An informal poll from the stores.org web site says 42 percent of clothing buyers *never* find clothes to fit; 40 percent only *sometimes*; 14 percent said *rarely* and only 4 percent said *always.*

In the movie, *The Devil Wears Prada*, Andy Sachs, the main character said she is a size 6, but her mentor declared that size "6 is the new 14." What *is* a 6, and what *is* a 14? Why is a size 4 in one designer label equivalent to a size 6 in another, and can be a 10 somewhere else? I have clients who have at minimum three sizes of garments handing in their closets. Doesn't this make you wonder: Is there any logic to sizes, or are they just a random jumble of numbers?

If finding your size seems more difficult than ever, or if you wonder why your size varies from manufacturer to manufacturer, let me assure you that the problem is not you. A 1999 study by Salmon Associates showed that 62 percent of U.S. consumers are dissatisfied with the fit of their apparel. This can be partially attributed to the outdated sizing standards, based on decades-old data, used by apparel manufacturers to create patterns. This U.S. Department of Commerce guideline, created in 1941, is based on an average woman who was 5' 2," weighing 129 pounds. Today, according to the National Center for Health Statistics, the average woman is 5' 4" and weighs 163 pounds (wearing between a size 12 and 14).

In addition, each designer or manufacturer has their *ideal* woman with specific height, weight, age, bust, waist, and hip measurements. Their designs fit *their* proportions, not necessarily ours. There is no standard of sizing among manufacturers, adding to the confusion for the consumer. Each style is produced to fit a range of bodies in an acceptable manner. Some clothes are baggy, so it can fit many bodies with little difference. Stretchy fabrics can also fit a wider range of bodies. A manufacturer's *goal* is to fit as many of us within a size as possible. And this does not mean fit *well*. I've heard someone say ready-to-wear is *almost ready-to-wear*, since it almost never fits perfectly without at least some minor alterations.

As fashion changes, so do acceptable standards of good fit. How clothes fit today is very different from how clothes fit five, ten or thirty years ago. Annie Brumbaugh, a New York-based wardrobe stylist and an AICI Certified Image Professional says, "Fit is probably the most critical issue in purchasing a garment. The most wonderful garment ever made by mankind will not look good if it doesn't fit." Another AICI associate, Judith Rasband, an AICI Certified Image Master, says "Fit can be more important than style, fabric, color, construction or price." The tip here is to look at the fit of the garment, not the size label.

Why A Good Fit Is Important

Fit is the most important aspect of purchasing a garment, because no matter the quality, label, or how much you spend, a poor-fitting garment will never look good. Therefore, you will never feel comfortable wearing it. If you put on a garment that is too tight, not only will you feel it being too tight, the garment also looks too tight, like you're trying to squeeze into the wrong size. If a garment is too loose, it will look baggy, and will give the appearance that a) it doesn't fit well, b) you look sloppy, or c) you're wearing someone else's clothes.

Good fit is characterized by clothing that skims the outline of your shape. Nothing clings or pulls, nor is anything so oversized that it hides your body's natural outline. When trying on a garment, ask yourself: Is anything pulling, puckering, gapping or bagging? Fit is also a very personal thing. I have clients who like their clothes to hug their body, so that they are close and tight. I have other clients who like to wear their clothes very loose and want extra ease in their waistbands, so that they have room to sit or not feel tight after they eat. Understanding how you want your clothes to "feel" can help you articulate to your tailor or alterations specialist the kinds of alterations you prefer.

Understanding Ease

Ease is the difference between your body measurements and your garment measurements. The amount of ease you may find comfortable is another personal preference. Minimum ease is the amount of fullness a designer or manufacturer allows for wearing comfort or "wiggle room." It is the excess amount found in a fitted garment made from a woven, not stretch fabric. A general guide for minimum ease is as follows:

Bust: 2"–3"   Hip: 1 ½"–3"
Waist: 1"–1 ½"   Upper Arm: 1 ½"

Design ease is the amount of fullness added to a garment in addition to minimum ease to achieve a fashion silhouette. Think of the difference between the fit of a dolman-sleeve top and a fitted shirt: the dolman sleeve has an exaggerated fullness around the arm's bicep area, whereas the fitted shirt would barely skim the arm area.

Body Types, Proportion and Fabrics

Another key to understanding good fit is being aware of body types and proportions—specifically yours. This will help you in choosing garments that work for your height and body proportion, taking into consideration your particular body challenges. See Elaine Stoltz's chapter in this book, "Embrace Your Body to Enhance Your Image."

A suit need not be expensive to look good. An inexpensive suit can look just fine if it is made well and if it fits (or can be made to fit) as if it were made for you. Here's what to look for.

Check proportion in a traditional men's suit: the measurement from the top of the collar to the hem of the jacket should equal that from the jacket hem to the bottom of the trousers. Proportion is less precise with a woman's suit. Depending on fashion, hemlines have their ups and downs for jackets, skirts, and pants. With a plain straight skirt, length is a matter of preference; but skirts with pleats, sizeable pockets or unusual details may lose proportion if the length is changed radically.

Fabric is crucial. How the fabric drapes and how the suit conforms to your body has a lot to do with how the fabric is cut. If you find a diagonal ripple halfway down the back of the jacket, the fabric probably wasn't cut on the grain; no amount of pressing will ever make the jacket hang properly.

Understanding how fabric must complement and support a body silhouette is also important. For example, a skirt made from cotton denim will be stiff and firm-looking, whereas a flared skirt made of chiffon will flow and hang softly. Pay close attention to the surface quality of fabrics, since weaves that add texture to a garment can also add "weight" to certain parts of the body that may not require any additional bulk. For example, with a fine merino wool sweater versus a fuzzy mohair sweater, the mohair will appear more bulky. The difference between a matte jersey and a high sheen satin jersey is that the shiny jersey will make the wearer look bigger, because of the sheen of the fabric—shiny fabrics tend to reflect instead of recede.

High quality clothes are a condition of excellence. In fashion, that translates to top-grade fabrics, superior workmanship and excellent design. Your average low-end to moderate mass merchandise is manufactured as inexpensively as possible with most garments designed to appeal to most of the people most of the time. Drape, fit, silhouette, fine detailing, and elegance are not high priorities. Knowing how a garment is constructed is also important in understanding fit. In today's market, you can find garments made with three basic techniques:

- ✦ Custom-tailored garments are made using a labor intensive, hand-stitched construction, with all the interfacings and padding hand-stitched together.

- ✦ Manufacturers of high- to mid-priced garments use the machine method, where instead of stitching by hand, everything is stitched with a sewing machine.

- ✦ The last method is the fusible method, where the interfacing is fused or glued to the fashion fabric to give it body and support. Most of the garments manufactured today use the fusible method. It is less labor intensive and quicker to produce than either of the other two methods.

Why should you care how something is constructed? Knowing how a garment is constructed will help you determine how to care for the garment. A jacket that uses the fusible method will not last as long as a jacket constructed by the custom method. The fusing will not hold up with multiple trips to the dry cleaners and will bubble and make your garment look uneven. Therefore, if you can purchase the best quality garment within your budget, you will have a garment that will last longer and in the long run, save you money.

Guidelines to Achieve a Good Fit

When we analyze fit for a jacket, we always start at the shoulders. The shoulders must sit perfectly straight and should balance on the shoulder without any drag or pull. A classic fit has the shoulder seam falling between ¼ to ½ inch outside the shoulder, but fashion may dictate otherwise. Shoulder seams that are too long make the garment feel and look sloppy. Alterations on shoulder seams are not easy, but it can be done.

The shoulder seam and the grain of the sleeves should line up perfectly. Any pull across the shoulder means that the jacket is too small. If you can't reach forward or move your arms over your head without feeling pressure in the chest, try the next size or a different cut. Be sure to check the width of your sleeves: a sleeve that is too wide can make you look bigger and bulkier than you are. If you have the sleeves tapered slightly, it'll make a huge difference in how the jacket looks and how you feel in it.

Do vertical seams in your garment hang straight, without pulling? Do you have an excess of fabric around the body or does it pull too tight due to not enough fabric? The body of your jacket should fit without clinging. A fit that is too snug creates horizontal lines across the back, pulls at the hips and may open the back vents. Button the jacket and raise and lower your arms, making sure that the jacket falls back into place without needing to readjust. Make sure there is ample room in the armholes for movement. Any curve at the waist of the jacket should be smooth. Often, higher-end garments offer a wider seam allowance, making it easier to let out seams for additional ease and comfort. Be sure to check the inside seams (if you can) to determine if this type of alteration can be performed.

If the garment has a bust line dart, does the stitched line point to the fullest area of the bust? Is this point one inch away from the apex - the fullest part of the bust? Are there excessive puckers at the point of a hip dart? If yes, the dart length needs to be lengthened. If you have a full bust, sometimes darts can be added to the garment to help this area fit better.

Don't underestimate the importance of properly fitted undergarments. A well-fitted bra can provide the foundation and structure needed for garments to hang smoothly. Many good department stores have fit specialists and hold bra clinics to help you find the correct size and style that works for your body shape. For more on this important topic see Bianca Stark-

Falcone's chapter, "Foundation Pieces: The Secret Behind Every Beautiful Curve."

Check the relationship of the button placements to the buttonholes. Does the closure have adequate ease or is there gapping and pulling? If yes, then small snaps can be placed between the buttonholes for added security. Does your zipper zip easily without stress?

The collar should hit near the middle of the neck without standing away from it. There should be no fabric bunching up underneath the collar. Medium lapels are the classic style and should be approximately 2 ½ inches wide. Each lapel should sit against the body and begin to roll just above the uppermost button. If the lapels gape, the jacket is too small in the chest area. When your jacket is buttoned, you should be able to sit comfortably. If a jacket is too tight an "X" pattern of pulled fabric will form over the closed buttons.

Bend your arm to check the length of the sleeves. When your hands hang at the sides, the sleeves should just cover your wrist bone. They should always taper towards your wrist. When you look at the hem from the side, it should be straight all around, with no dipping front or back. When your arms are folded, is the garment comfortable across the back or is it straining or sagging at the shoulder?

Pockets should lie closed without any gaps or pulling. If they gap, the garment is too tight or too low. Most pockets can be removed and stitched closed to prevent gapping and extra width.

Skirt hems should fall equally all the way around the circumference of the hem. The lower edge should be parallel to the floor. Linings should not hang below the outer layer. The sides of skirts can sometimes be tapered to maintain proper proportions. It is important to discover the *best* length for your leg.

The easiest way to determine the hem length of a skirt is to stand sideways in front of a full-length mirror, and pull the skirt up, just below the thickest part of the leg. The best point will not be the same for everyone. A short skirt should fall before the calf starts to widen; a mid-length skirt should never end at the middle of the calf, but just below where the calf starts to narrow. Also consider how the skirt will look when you are seated. In many instances, a straight or tight skirt will pull up more than expected.

Fitting pants can be tricky, as most of us have more than one area of fit challenges with pants. In front of a full-length mirror, examine your pants from every angle. How do they feel? Are there wrinkles? Are the side seams straight and perpendicular to the floor? Here are some typical signs and the areas that may require adjustments:

- "Smile" lines from the front crotch area, radiating across the thighs—full thighs
- Crotch area feels too tight, high or low—crotch length
- Horizontal wrinkles from the back crotch—full thighs or large seat
- Wrinkles below the back waistband—sloping back waistline
- Side seams pitch forward—swayback
- Side seams swing backward—full high hip and posture
- Tightness around thigh or calves—not enough fabric in these areas
- Vertical wrinkles under the seat—flat derriere

When to Alter

The more a garment cost originally, the more sense it makes to invest in alterations. Also, figure how much you would have to pay for a new skirt (or jacket or pants) of similar quality. If it's more than it will cost to fix the old, altering is worth it. Here are some common alterations:

+ Lengthening or shortening pants or skirt hems
+ Shortening or lengthening sleeves
+ Taking in side seams on jackets, pants, or skirts
+ Tapering sleeves
+ Tapering pant legs and skirts
+ Letting out waistbands
+ Taking in waistbands (for pants, no more than 2 inches)
+ Enlarging armholes on vests, shirts and jackets)
+ Adding shoulder pads

These alterations are considered more difficult, meaning that they take more time and are more complicated:

+ Taking in a shoulder line
+ Raising the shoulder in jackets, dresses, blouses and shirts
+ Taking in or letting out the center back of jackets
+ Shortening the rise in pants
+ Shortening coat length

When Not to Alter

+ When a garment requires extensive alterations
+ Satin and moiré fabrics leave holes when altered
+ Velvet, suede cloth, and corduroy will show marks, so they can be taken in, but not let out
+ Plaid, striped and checkered fabrics
+ Clothing that does not have enough seam allowance
+ If you've lost more than 35 pounds, it's better to purchase a new garment

Final Tips on Fit

+ **Find a good tailor or alterations specialist.** This person can be your lifesaver. This may not be your local dry cleaners, not to say that they can't do an adequate job, but if you have expensive garments that require special attention, my recommendation would be to take it to a specialist.

+ **Invest in a good clothing steamer** as a good alternative to dry cleaning. Using a steamer is five times faster than ironing. You can also get those wrinkles out quickly, plus you can steam while the garment is still on the hanger. An added bonus is that steamers also eliminate odors, because the steam kills the odor-causing bacteria. You can purchase a steamer from www.jiffysteamer.com and use my promo code "Image130" to receive free shipping. The most popular model is the Esteam Travel®. I personally love the J-2000M residential model for all other steaming needs.

+ **Have a small toolbox** that has needles, threads, and a small pair of scissors. Use a small Ziploc® bag to hold any threads or buttons that come with your sweater, shirt, jacket, or coat purchases. Staple them to the price tag and write a quick description of what it belongs to.

* **Don't wait until the last minute** to have your garments altered. At the beginning of each season, make sure all your items are ready to wear, alleviating the stress of having things done at the last minute.

* **Expect to pay for alterations**—it is well worth the money. Whether the garment is expensive or not, if it is well-tailored and fits you properly, you'll look and feel like a million bucks! On the other hand, whether it's expensive or not, if it doesn't fit, it will look awful and cheap.

Take the time to become more knowledgeable about how clothing fits your body. You will derive great benefit from this understanding. Not only will you be able to make better choices in your clothing selection, but will save money in the long run by knowing what to avoid. Your clothing is a resource—a tool that will help you meet your current needs and accomplish your long-range goals. Let your wardrobe work as hard as you do to achieve your personal and professional objectives.

HELENA CHENN, AICI CIP
Helena Chenn Designs

*A custom design and
wardrobe management company*

**(408) 973-9045
hc@helenachenn.com
www.helenachenn.com**

Helena is a wardrobe expert and image consultant, an industry leader in the field of wardrobe styling and fit. Her specialties include: comprehensive wardrobe design for private clients, complete closet organization, professional personal shopping, and exceptional tailoring and alterations for both men and women. Helena believes that you should use your clothing as a resource—a vital tool that will help you feel good about yourself and project the image you want to the world.

Helena is in demand as a workshop leader, giving in-depth scrutiny and analysis on every aspect of wardrobe planning and image management. An active member of the prestigious Association of Image Consultants International (AICI), a worldwide non-profit professional association specializing in visual appearance, verbal and non-verbal communications, she has received their highest accolades including: The IMMIE Award of Excellence and the AICI Award of Excellence. She is a two-time recipient of the AICI San Francisco Bay Area Chapter's Member of the Year Award. Helena is also a member of the Association of Design & Sewing Professionals (ADSP) and the American Sewing Guild (ASG).

Accessories:
The Frosting of Fashion

How to Add the Finishing Touches to Your Wardrobe

By Marjory DeRoeck, MFA, AICI CIP

Every woman deserves attention and admiration. If you have a workable wardrobe but still feel like a wallflower at the dance, then an accessory overhaul might just be what you need. Often my image clients have told me it was difficult for them to choose the right accessories. "What size, what color, what shape, what style?" Since they were not able to figure it out on their own, they wore no accessories at all. Don't follow that path! By the time you have finished reading this chapter you will have the tools to create a sensational accessory wardrobe. Just a word of warning: be prepared for the compliments that will be coming your way.

Your Personal Statement

Accessories provide a fun and inexpensive way to create excitement in your wardrobe. They add the little often-overlooked touches that turn an expected look into a delightful surprise. Accessories will allow you to make a personal statement about who you are.

*"I should like my dress to be a poem about myself, my 'persona,'
the outward and visible presentation of my individuality."*
– Pall Mall Gazette (1884)

I have a dear friend who loves country-style décor. The prints, colors, and textures of her clothing and accessories also reflect this love. Whenever I see a whimsical wooden pin, hand-painted necklace or patchwork shawl, I think of her. She knows how to express her inner self and people are drawn to her sincerity and charm.

Any add-on that you use to enhance or complete an outfit is considered an accessory. Many items fall into this category. They include:

For upper body emphasis:

- Jewelry
- Scarves
- Shawls, capes and wraps
- Hats
- Watches
- Eyeglasses

For lower body emphasis:

- Belts
- Hosiery
- Shoes
- Handbags fall into the neutral range
- Makeup and nail polish

Some of these items will be discussed in other chapters of this book, so I will concentrate on helping you discover the wonderful world of accessory basics.

Top Reasons to Use Accessories

+ **To put separates together as outfits.** Use a multicolored scarf as a roadmap to pull together individual clothing items. A brown, orange and gold scarf would coordinate with brown pants, an orange sweater and a gold tee.

- **To direct attention toward your best features.** Is a tiny waist one of your best assets? Wear a wide leather belt with a gorgeous buckle and everyone will notice.

- **To vary your wardrobe to suit your mood.** Feeling upbeat? Put on your sparkly earrings. Feeling calm and casual? Add a mohair scarf in your eye color.

- **To provide a conversation piece.** Attach an interesting pin on your lapel and see how many people comment. It's a great icebreaker at a party.

- **To add color to your neutral color garments.** Neutral colors are less memorable and can drain color from your skin. Add a scarf or necklace in a complementary color to draw attention to your face.

- **To extend your wardrobe.** Bring a dress or suit out of your closet and try adding groupings of accessories. Each time you make a change, the cost per wearing of the dress or suit goes down because you have more ways to wear it. Now that's what I call cost effective.

- **To update an older garment.** Take an old blazer, pair it with great fitting, dark denim jeans, a lacy cami, drop-dead metallic shoes and dangle earrings, and watch heads turn when you walk into a restaurant. At that rate, your blazer could last you another couple of years.

- **To pull together unusual color combinations.** Being a redhead, I have a lot of green and turquoise in my wardrobe. I never put the colors together until I found a summer handbag that combined both colors. Now I have extended my summer wardrobe without buying any new clothes.

- **To express your creativity.** To me, this is the most important reason to bring accessories into your wardrobe—and into your life. Often my clients have said,

"But I'm not creative." I say, "Yes you are." Maybe you just haven't had time to develop this special gift. Start noticing the colors, shapes and textures around you. What do you find pleasing to your eyes? Look through magazines for new ideas. Tear them out and make a collage by gluing them onto a piece of poster board. Now you'll start recognizing the style elements that you prefer.

Remember, accessories always make dressing easier, more cost-effective, and FUN.

"Know, first, who you are; and then adorn yourself accordingly."
– Epictetus, Greek Stoic philosopher

Know Who You Are Before Shopping

As you delve deeper into the world of accessories, here are some guidelines to keep in mind:

- **Complement your face shape and skin texture.** Examine your face in the mirror. Are your features angular or curved? Is your face long or round? It is most pleasing to mimic the inside lines of your face—the angles or curves—and balance the outside lines, using horizontal shapes if your face is long, and vertical shapes if your face is wide. If your skin is smooth and creamy, opt for smooth textured jewelry and scarves. Natural beads and scarves made of natural fibers usually look more harmonious next to skin with freckles or a rougher texture.

- **Know your body shape.** Your accessories should carry the viewer's gaze along a vertical line. You can minimize your figure challenges and draw attention to your best features simply by placing an accessory where you want the viewer's eyes to rest. It is always best to place the most color or

design near your face to draw attention toward your face—
your "communication center."

+ **Emphasize your hair color.** One of the best tips I can
give you is to buy some great accessories in your hair color.
This is a basic rule I give to all my clients. Include a quality
handbag, a belt, and several styles of shoes in your hair
color. Classic styles go with everything in your wardrobe
and can last for years. Once you have these basic items, opt
for beads, earrings and scarves that include this color.

If your hair color is:	Buy leather items in:
Warm Blonde	Camel or Cream
Cool Blonde	Taupe
Red	Rust
Warm Brown	Chocolate Brown
Cool Brown	Rose Brown or Brown-Black
Grey	Charcoal
Black or Very Dark Brown	Black

+ **Discover your personal style.** You will read much more
about personal style in Cheri Bertelsen's chapter, "Find
Your Unique Personal Style." However, since it is of vital
importance when choosing your accessories, I will briefly
review the styles. Personal style is your inner personality
brought to the outside. It is a way you can create a look
that is uniquely you. Alyce Parson's Universal Style
System™ lists the basic styles as sporty, traditional, and
elegant, and accent styles as feminine, alluring, creative,
and dramatic. Each style has its own accessory personality.
Let's examine them briefly.

Sporty: Fun, whimsical accessories. Hoop or ball earrings.
Pearl necklace or earthy pendant on a chain or cord. A short

neckerchief worn around the neck, around a ponytail or on the handle of a handbag. Comfortable shoes and practical handbags in natural materials.

Traditional: Classic, toned down accessories. Button earrings, 24-inch bead or pearl necklaces, classic pins. Silk scarves worn inside the neck of a suit jacket. Closed toed, solid color pumps or walking shoes. Medium sized, functional shoulder bags in quality leather.

Elegant: Smooth, pared down, coordinated accessories. Matching earrings and necklaces. Multiple strands of pearls or chains. Elegant silk scarves. Sling back or classic shoes in smooth, fine leather. Structured bags of high quality leather and status materials. Designer labels.

Feminine: Romantic accessories. Small, openwork or clustered earrings. Dainty, delicate necklaces. Lacey, openwork pins. Loose, flowing scarves. Belts in soft leathers or fabrics tied as a sash or bow. Curved and unstructured bags in soft materials.

Alluring: Seductive accessories. Earrings are hoops or dangles with lots of movement. Necklaces and pendants fit the cleavage of the bust. Scarves are worn at the waist or hip. Shoes have open designs with straps, or low cut lines and high heels. Wide, soft belts show off the waist.

Creative: Surprising, eclectic accessories. Multiple earrings of different styles worn in one ear. Unusual necklaces in a wide variety of materials, often mixed together. Pins worn in unexpected places. Large shawls draped across the shoulders or body, or tied at the hip. Low, comfortable shoes or boots. Medium-to-large fabric or soft leather bags or backpacks.

Dramatic: Bold accessories that make a statement. Oversized earrings, often geometric in design. Sculpted necklaces in quality metals. Statement brooches with abstract designs. Scarves in bold, contrasting colors worn asymmetrically on the body. Shoes are sleek and angular. Bags are structured and large.

- **Know your best colors.** If you have not had your coloring analyzed or if you had it done more than 15 years ago, I encourage you to have a color analysis consultation. Knowing your best colors will save you time and money while shopping and allow you to coordinate your accessories with your clothing selections.

There are variations between color analysis systems. However, most agree that your skin, hair, and eye colors are the clues to deciding your best accessory, as well as your best wardrobe, colors.

If you have warm coloring, you will look wonderful in colors with yellow undertones: red orange, yellow green, aqua, rust, avocado, peach, and coral. You will be particularly drawn toward gold, copper and bronze metals.

If you have cool coloring, you will look best in blue-undertoned colors: royal blue, rose, blue red, magenta, wine, plum, and hunter green. Your best metals are silver, platinum, pewter and light gold.

Still not sure what colors are best for you? Then simply look at your hair and eye colors for accessory clues. As I previously mentioned, purchasing basic leather accessories in your hair color is of great benefit. Necklaces, earrings, and scarves in your eye color will also bring attention to your face. Wearing your eye color makes you appear more believable and trustworthy and can have a calming influence on those around you.

Okay, I know some of you are saying, "But what if I have plain brown eyes?" Believe me, brown is not just brown. You probably have a glint of yellow or red or green within the brown and that's the color you can repeat. Also, if you desire additional color variety, look at a color wheel in a paint or art store and find the complementary color to your eyes. That is the color that is opposite your eye color on the color wheel. I have a client who has green-brown eyes and I suggested she wear a purple scarf. For the first time, people started noticing her eyes and giving her compliments. What a boost to her self esteem!

The Importance of Scale and Balance

Your bone structure, height and weight are also important determining factors in the size of the accessories you choose. Here is an overview of scale and balance:

+ **Small Scale.** Your wrist measures 5½ inches or smaller, you are quite slender and 5'7" or under in height. Your jewelry can be quite delicate and your scarf designs should be moderate to small. Be careful of large or overstuffed handbags as they can visually overwhelm you.

+ **Medium Scale.** Your wrist measures 5½ to 7½ inches, you are 5'4" or taller and are of moderate weight. Choose medium size earrings and necklaces or wear several strands of chains or beads. Small size accessories will make you look larger and large accessories can overwhelm you.

+ **Large Scale.** Your wrist measures 7½ inches or larger, you are 5'7" or taller and are medium or overweight. Experiment with singular, eye- catching brooches, fabulous shawls, bracelet cuffs, and medium-to-large handbags. Stay away from tiny stud earrings and small pendants with delicate chains.

A Few Words About Shoes

Whether you love designer shoes, and can afford them, or you are a sneaker kind of girl, my best advice is to *put comfort first*. Fortunately more and more shoe designers and companies are offering shoes with comfort insoles and a range of heel heights. There is no longer any reason for you to submit your tootsies to the torture of an uncomfortable or ill-fitting shoe. Here are a few shoe tips:

+ Shoe shop in the middle of the day. By then your feet have spread and you will be buying a more comfortable size.

+ Just as in clothing, shoe sizes are not all the same. Ask to have your feet measured before deciding on a size.

+ A quality, classic pump with a 2½-inch heel can last you for several years. Be sure you buy a pair in your hair color. I know—you've heard that before!

+ Look for styles that fit your personality. If you love your leather loafers, then you might feel foolish wearing shiny stiletto heels. But try them on anyway. You just might find that hidden Diva within you.

+ At the end of the day, polish or brush your shoes and let them air dry before storing.

"For a woman, the right shoe can make everything different. It can make you walk better, feel better."
– Jimmy Choo, footwear designer

The Art of Organizing

Now that you know how accessories can extend your wardrobe and add pizzazz to your appearance, here are the steps for organizing those special items.

- On a flat surface, like your bed or a table, lay out all your necklaces, earrings and bracelets. Eliminate any that are broken, the wrong color or metal, too small or too large in scale, or that you simply do not like. Gather the remaining pieces into combinations of similar colors and styles.

- Take out your belts, shoes, and handbags. You probably didn't realize you had so many! Eliminate those that are worn beyond repair, hurt your feet, don't fit your personal style, or look outdated. Be sure you have one of each item—say it with me—in your hair color.

- Take all your scarves out of your drawers. Eliminate those you dislike and arrange the remaining ones on scarf hangers. My favorite hanger is from the Container Store. It is a plastic, solid coat hanger with 24 holes through which you can thread your scarves. You can hang it in your closet next to your jackets.

- If possible, store your shoes and handbags on shelves in your closet or in a separate dresser or armoire. Put the handbags individually in old pillowcases or cloth bags. Avoid storing shoes at the bottom of your closet. This area is visually dark, can become dusty, and your shoes or boots can rub against your clothing and each other. And that's no way to treat your Jimmy Choos!

- Lastly, create capsules with your accessories. You already know to bring together jewelry, a scarf, shoes, belt, and a bag in your hair color. Do the same with your eye color. Take some of your favorite accent colors and develop accessory groupings that will give punch to your basic wardrobe. Don't forget your favorite metallic items, too. Depending on your coloring, a capsule of gold, bronze, copper, silver or pewter will work with almost everything in your wardrobe. If you don't think you'll remember what you've grouped together, take a picture of each collection.

Put the pictures in a small photo album or, if you're really feeling creative, incorporate them into a framed collage.

My motto for accessory storage is, "If you can see it, then you'll wear it." Put your wonderfully creative mind to work. Imagine an area of your bedroom or bathroom where you could display your accessories. You might attach your pins to a velvet ribbon and hang it on the wall. I have a client who puts her flower pins on a small French bulletin board—the kind that is padded and has ribbon criss-crossing diagonally over it. Many decorative earring holders will attach to the wall and have spaces for 30 or more pairs as well as knobs for hanging chains and necklaces. Who needs pictures on the wall when you have beautiful accessories to display.

If you have limited space, consider a jewelry armoire. The sides will swing open to hold necklaces and, in the velvet-lined drawers, you can nestle your favorite rings, bracelets, pendants, and earrings. Just remember not to crowd the jewelry. You don't want tangled chains and scratched metal.

Accessory Wisdom

I firmly believe that a well-dressed woman should spend at least one third of her wardrobe budget on accessories and the remainder on clothing items. The advice I give my clients is, "Never purchase a new outfit without buying the accessories to go with it." If you get home and find you don't have the right shoes, or necklace, or belt to complete the outfit, then you've just wasted time having to go back to the store. If you don't want to buy the accessories for an outfit, then you don't love the outfit enough.

Okay, so now you are dressed and ready to go. You take one last look in your full-length mirror. (You do have one, don't you?) What's missing? Nothing! You have followed the tips I've given you. You realize how accessories can stretch your wardrobe, how your coloring can affect your choices, and how being true to your personal style boosts your confidence. You've put together several accessory capsules and love each item. Now you're ready to step out into the world with style and confidence. Your accessories are a reflection of your own unique beauty. Listen to the compliments, smile, and just say "thank you."

MARJORY DEROECK, MFA, AICI CIP
All About Image

Develop a new view of you!

(925) 299-0660
marjory@theimagestudio.biz
www.theimagestudio.biz

When Marjory discovered image consulting she knew it would be a natural blend of her creative energy and teaching expertise. She specializes in color analysis, makeup application, accessorizing, and personal style. Her studio is an elegant space where clients feel relaxed and pampered. The studio includes a makeup area, dressing room, accessory boutique, and space for teaching image classes.

Marjory particularly enjoys working with mature women who want to continue looking current and fashionable in styles and colors appropriate for their lifestyle. She also likes working with pre and post-op plastic surgery clients to help them achieve a beautiful visual impact.

In the business world, Marjory is a past president of The Women's Network of Contra Costa County, Director of Women's Business Connection of LaMorinda and Northern California Regional trainer for Beauty For All Seasons. She is an active member of AICI and has earned Certified Image Professional (CIP) status. She has served as AICI San Francisco Bay Area Chapter Co-President and is currently Co-VP of Education.

LOOK As Good As You SEE

Choosing Eyewear to Frame Your Image

By Wendy Buchanan, AICI, LO

Research tells us how important the visual element is to human perception. In fact, 55 percent of a first impression is formed through visual communication. With three out of four people in need of prescription lenses, eyewear has become a common aspect of personal style and image. In the 30 seconds we have to make a first impression, eye contact is a critical component of the interaction—just as important as our smile. I like to say that people who meet you for the first time look at three things: first your smile, then your eyes (and eyewear), and then your shoes!

Eyewear used to be seen merely as a medical device to correct a visual impairment. No consideration was given to how the glasses looked—only that they were compatible with the prescription requirements and perhaps that they were comfortable. No wonder people were ashamed to wear glasses as recently as a generation ago. Eyeglasses were seen as something that announced and emphasized a defect.

How times have changed! The exact opposite is true today, and even people who do not require prescription lenses choose to wear eyeglass frames for professional reasons or to enhance their style. Today, eyewear is a key element of total image that can help you express who you are. It can become a signature item and a clever business tool. It can also be a fun fashion accessory that is changed for different outfits and occasions.

There is both an art and a science to choosing eyewear that looks great, feels right and functions to suit one's lifestyle. What you wear projects your image, but it is the accessories we choose that truly convey personality. As one of the most noticeable accessories we will ever wear, eyeglasses help to complete a total image. Eyewear not only influences the way we see but also the way others see us.

Many individuals wear eyeglasses every day, all day. Although we would never wear the same clothing, shoes or belt seven days a week, many people have only one pair of glasses. Empowering individuals to use their eyewear as a key aspect of their images and personalities is my passion. Just as we choose our clothing based on our agenda and goals for the day, we can choose eyewear to meet our personal goals.

In my work, over more than a decade and working with hundreds of clients, I have witnessed how eyewear can help a person to:

- Improve business performance through greater confidence
- Get to the next interview phase in the job selection process by standing out from the ordinary and being memorable
- Gain an audience's attention because eyewear can help a person project a "take control" image
- Be perceived as more mature and credible in a new career
- Reflect his or her creativity through the choice of unique eyewear
- Be noticed when walking into a networking event

+ Create a marketing image around eyewear, even using eyewear as a "branding" piece for his or her individual or corporate brand

Confidence Booster

Some of my clients feel so much more confident wearing their glasses in business situations that they have eliminated contact lenses as an option for their business image. Just as external perceptions equate intelligence with eyewear, people who do wear glasses often feel smarter and more intellectual—and can project that outward. Time and again when a client tries on glasses, I often hear, "Wow, I look smart!" I have also witnessed clients' body language change simply as a result of wearing glasses and feeling that change in perception.

Case in point: One of my clients, Michelle, had been booked for her first television interview. It would be her first time on a live broadcast and she was a little intimidated by it. While she knew her business and her subject matter well, she felt she needed a boost of confidence to help her through this media attention. I fit her with non-prescription, blue cobalt eyeglasses to create an intellectual, powerful image so the audience would remember her and listen to her message, and so she would feel greater confidence. Michelle went on air to have a successful television interview that also generated leads for new business.

Standing Out from the Crowd

The interview process for a job can be a nerve-racking experience for the interviewee. It can also be a lengthy and intense process for the interviewer. How does one sift through all the applicants with various work experiences and skill sets to finally decide on the best person for the job? Eyewear can help a person to be more memorable than other job applicants, and to convey the right image for the position.

Case in point: After having been with the same company for 20 years in a technical customer support career, Peter was on the hunt for a new job and wanted to apply his skills to an outside-sales position that suited his extrovert personality. He wanted to update his image and have new eyeglasses to reflect where he saw himself going.

I changed Peter's eyewear from an understated, wire-rimmed, John-Lennon-style frame to a thick, rectangular metal frame. When he was called back for a second interview, he was told that he stood out from the other applicants because of his outgoing personality and his funky glasses. He got the job! "The glasses have helped me quote on more business," he says. "I look very distinguished, yet 'out there.' I always leave an impression on the client. Then I get to quote and make the sale."

A Dramatic Pause

Eyeglasses can be just as effective off the face as they are on the face. One of my clients is a lawyer. When she is in the courtroom and feels that the judge or the jury have started to tune her out, she will use her eyeglasses as a "tool" to capture their attention. She stops her dialogue and, in a swift movement, removes her glasses, holds them at her side for five seconds, then slowly and methodically puts the eyeglasses back on her face, all the while making eye contact with the jury. It's a piece of drama that works to regain her audience's attention.

Practical Considerations

Many people now need eyewear for reading, and for my clients who often speak in front of groups I always recommend progressive lenses as opposed to a pair of reading glasses. This allows a speaker to look from her speaking materials to her audience without having to adjust her glasses, which can become distracting and cause the audience to stop paying attention to the message. An audience may also perceive a speaker who is peering over her reading glasses as "speaking down" to them. We can all probably remember a teacher or principal who peered down at us while delivering a reprimand for some misunderstanding.

Personal Branding

Glasses can be a wonderful marketing tool. I have a client who owns a marketing company and gains a large percentage of her new business through networking. She believes her eyeglasses are a key part of her brand and a worthwhile business investment. We chose orange glasses with a wire rim that sweeps across the bottom, while the top of the frame is rimless. When she walks into a networking meeting, other business people notice her. She meets many new people simply because they are drawn to her eyewear and comment on the style and color. The glasses reflect her marketing creativity as well as her unique business model, creating a complete branding package.

Glasses Mean Business

While it may sound improbable that glasses can increase one's business, I have learned first-hand through many clients that it's literally true. From giving the wearer the confidence needed to deliver an effective television interview, to standing out enough to be remembered among a sea of job applicants, projecting the necessary image to close a deal, or being the reason a person approaches *you* at a networking event, well-chosen eyewear can have seriously positive results in business.

Fitting For Face Shapes

The primary goal of fitting eyewear for different face shapes is to achieve proportion and balance. My system is based on matching the client's face shape with the same or similar shape in eyeglass frames. By working with the natural curves or natural angles in the face, not only will the frame shape enhance their features, it will be a true reflection of who they are.

Face shapes fall into three categories, with a total of ten face shapes:

- **Balanced face shapes: Oval and Hexagon.** These two face shapes can wear many shapes of eyeglass frames. Balanced facial features have symmetry. The face may be slightly narrower at the jaw line than at the temples. Eyeglass frames should have soft curves for the oval face shape and strong angles for the hexagon face shape.

- **Curved face shapes: Oblong, Round, Teardrop, and Heart.** Curved facial features can include rounded eyes and cheeks, as well as curved lips and eyebrows. The forehead and chin are round and soft. Eyeglass frames for these face shapes will have soft lines, rounded corners and a curved frame shape.

- **Angular face shapes: Rectangle, Square, Triangle, and Diamond.** Angular facial features can include parallel lines at the nose, almond-shaped eyes and straight eyebrows. The forehead and jaw lines are square or pointed. Eyeglass frames for these face shapes will have straight lines, sharp angles and a geometric frame shape.

Fitting Goal for Oval and Hexagon Face Shapes: These face shapes have a natural facial balance and can easily wear many different shapes in eyeglass frames. Keep the frames in proportion to the face shape and keep the weight of the frame material in balance with bone structure and body type.

Oval

Hexagon

The fitting goals for Curved and Angular face shapes are similar, depending on the shape. For example:

Fitting Goal for Round and Square face shapes: to lengthen the face so it appears more oval or hexagon. Frames should be narrow and as wide as the face.

Round

Square

Curved Face Shape   Angular Face Shape

Fitting goal for Oblong and Rectangle face shapes: to shorten and widen the face. Frames should have a deep shape vertically and can be slightly wider than the face.

Oblong

Rectangle

Curved Face Shape   Angular Face Shape

Fitting goal for Heart and Triangle face shapes: to add width lower on the face. Eyeglasses are worn across the widest part of these two face shapes so the frame should avoid creating more width across the eyes. Frames are best in a uniform color, and design detail should be on the bottom of the frame only.

Heart

Triangle

Curved Face Shape   Angular Face Shape

Fitting Goal for Teardrop and Diamond face shapes: to add width across the forehead. Choose frames with a strong top bar and design details on the edge of the frame.

Teardrop

Diamond

Curved Face Shape   Angular Face Shape

Have an Eyewear Wardrobe

Just as our wardrobes change for the season, the occasion, or our moods, so should our eyewear. This accessory has emerged beyond a functional status symbol to an everyday must-have. We could not get by with one pair of shoes or carry one handbag, yet many would wear only one pair of eyeglasses for all occasions. To meet the needs of our multi-faceted lives and to complete our total image we need at least three pairs of eyeglasses: one pair for business dress, one pair for casual, relaxed attire, and one pair for sun protection.

With the expense of prescription lenses, eyeglasses can cost as much as a good suit but are an investment that you will wear far more often than any one suit. Eyewear is the one accessory that can add intelligence and credibility to our total look. In my experience over the last 11 years, I have seen that the return on investment can be significant.

When eyeglass frames are matched to your face shape, personality, and wardrobe, they will become an accessory that will have you *looking as good as you see* for many years. No longer will you buy a new pair of eyeglasses and file the old pair in a drawer—you will expand your collection and build a wardrobe of eyewear. Perhaps one day, more of us will have a room specifically to display our eyewear—just like Elton John.

WENDY BUCHANAN, AICI, LICENSED OPTICIAN
Perceptions Eyewear, Inc.

Your mobile eyewear boutique™

(905) 785-9668
wendy@perceptionseyewear.com
www.perceptionseyewear.com

Wendy Buchanan is the "Eyewear Image Expert" and founder of Perceptions Eyewear, Inc. As a licensed optician and image consultant, Wendy combined her two passions with her keen sense of style and "fun loving" personality to offer an entirely unique personalized service for eyewear consumers: helping them to LOOK as good as they SEE. Wendy caters to busy professionals who want their eyewear to enhance their business image, accessorize their wardrobes and reflect their unique personalities.

After a ten-year career as a licensed optician in a traditional optical store, Wendy launched her trademarked mobile eyewear boutique in 1997. Wendy offers a one-of-a-kind mobile service meeting her clients right at their home or office. In a one-hour appointment, Wendy assesses the client's face shape, clothing style, career, and personality, and helps them select the perfect eyewear to create their personal WOW factor.

In 2008, Wendy was nominated for the Canadian Women Entrepreneur of the Year Award. Wendy has also developed the training system, "Get Framed - Choosing Eyewear to Frame Your Image," a unique system of matching eyewear to an individual based on face shape, wardrobe style, and personality.

Makeup Techniques, Tips and Tools

Easy Steps to the Most Beautiful You

By Molly Klipp

Be Who You Were Meant to Be—
Enhance Your Natural Beauty

No matter our age, most of us are either trying to look older or younger, hip or classy, natural or glamorous. The fun thing is that depending on the situation, you can be any of these things.

We all have the ability to be creative. Use your mind, your vision, and your abilities to enjoy color, style, fashion, and of course, makeup—which is the icing on the cake for whatever look you are seeking.

Makeup at one time was face paint to be worn by ladies of the evening and older women trying to look younger, or as a cover up for imperfections of the skin. We've come a long way, baby! Thank goodness! Today, makeup is a relatively easy way to help you achieve the look you desire. This chapter is all about the techniques you use to achieve that look. It really is simple and easy and you can look great in just five to ten minutes.

We all know why we wear makeup; we want to achieve a particular look. What I am going to share with you are products, applications, and tips that help you personalize your makeup look. Embrace this information. Learn more about it and how it works for you. Makeup is not a tattoo or permanent, it is washable and changeable.

The key is to try different styles, techniques, and colors until you find the ones you like. Pick up some of the tips from this chapter and see if they work for you. Share them with a friend and let her try them out. Experiment and above all, have fun!

Do you want to look like a cover girl from a top fashion magazine, just a subtler version? Great! That's exactly what you will be learning in the next few pages. It's the proper techniques, the tips, secrets of the trade so to speak, and the magic tools—the brushes, sponges, and colors—that bring makeup alive.

Five Steps to Begin Your Journey to the Most Beautiful You

1. Skin care is always the first step to a great makeup look. No amount of makeup can hide a poorly cared-for complexion. Take great care of your skin and your makeup will always look better.
2. Wash your makeup off every night before you go to bed. If you don't, your sleep isn't beauty sleep—it is the equivalent of aging your skin seven days while you sleep.
3. Be sure to moisturize before applying makeup. It stays on longer and comes off easier.

4. Have the proper makeup tools before you begin: sponges, brushes, makeup remover, eyelash curler, cotton swabs, and proper lighting.

5. Choose the proper colors of foundation, powder, blush, eye shadows, eyeliners, mascara, eyebrow liners, lip liners, and lip colors for you.

Here's How to Create a More Fabulous You with Makeup

Concealer. A good concealer is your first step. It should be a tone slightly lighter than your own skin tone. But too light a concealer will throw off your whole makeup look. If you have very dark circles under your eyes, a darker concealer works better than a lighter concealer to hide them. Four things will cause dark circles:

+ Not drinking enough water

+ Not getting enough sleep

+ Extreme weight loss, which can leave fatty pockets under the skin around the eye area and cause dark circles

+ Genes—your family has them and has lovingly handed them down to you. Lucky you! The best thing to do is to pay attention to the first two things in the above list to help avoid a really bad case of dark circles. Then use a darker concealer to help hide them and use loose powder to smooth them out.

Foundation is used only to even out skin tones and to cover up imperfections of the skin. If you have good, even skin tones avoid using foundation at all. Keep your skin looking as natural as you can for as long as you can. Let's take a look at the different kinds of foundation—crème-to-powder, mineral powder foundation and liquid foundation—in terms of which might be best for your skin.

Crème to Powder is great for normal to dry skin and has great coverage with a makeup sponge. Make sure you match to your skin tone as best you can.

Mineral Powder Foundation is great for all skin types and is easy to apply. Use a chisel brush or sponge for application. This foundation can be used for full to minimal coverage. It's great for beginners and women who want it easy and natural because it's the most versatile and easiest to apply. It's quick, too. Pur Minerals® has a great formula; Aloette Cosmetics® has a similar product at a better price.

Liquid Foundation. This type of foundation is the most popular with Baby Boomers because it is familiar and has great coverage.

Apply foundation on the forehead and cheekbones, and always blend foundation and color down following the natural hair follicles. You may apply foundation all over the face and the eyelid area for a better overall makeup look. Blend into sheer coverage along the jaw line and smooth under the chin. Never take foundation down the neck. This technique avoids those terrible "panty lines" of improperly applied makeup. You've seen them, and don't you just want to go "fix their face?"

After using liquid foundation, use a translucent powder for easier blending and application of cheek and eye color.

Aloette Cosmetics has great light liquid foundations for a natural look. Prescriptives® Cosmetics has a great formula with heavier coverage and will mix a personalized color just for you if needed.

Getting the Right Foundation Color

When matching your foundation to your skin tone always check whatever foundation you are using along the jaw line of your face. Be sure not to use your hand or the inside of your wrist for matching colors because it is not accurate. The color must blend both with your face skin tone and your neck skin tone to avoid "panty lines" on your face. Use great makeup sponges that are washable and reusable. Aloette has the best sponges I have seen and they are very inexpensive and washable.

Getting That "Tan" Look Without Sun or Tanning Products
When summer comes and you want to add "color" to your face without changing foundation colors, try this. Purchase a liquid bronzer if you are using liquid foundation or a powder bronzer if using mineral powder foundation and mix the bronzer with your normal foundation to create a more natural "glowing" look. The amount you mix will depend on how much color you want to add to your skin tone. This looks natural and it won't damage your skin like the sun will! Again, be sure to blend carefully on the neck to avoid that "panty line."

Cheek Color

Choosing the right color and making the proper application frames your eyes to their best advantage. Cheek color should be applied no higher than the lower eye socket bone, no lower than the contour line below the cheekbone, and no closer than two fingers to the nose. When working on this technique, think of a fish face as you suck your cheeks in. Apply from the cheek bone and go back to the hairline in a downward stroke. Blend with a makeup sponge to make it look natural. Blending is the single most important key to a fabulous makeup look.

Eye Shadow Color

Select two to three colors, colors that will complement your clothing ensemble. Makeup is an accessory, just like earrings or a necklace. Choose medium, dark, and light colors. You can use any combination of colors together. It's the blending with the brushes that makes it look natural and beautiful. Follow these three steps in order:

- Medium shade (can use lighter shade for this too) is applied with an eye shadow brush all over the lid and lightly under the brow.

- Darker shade is applied with a contour brush starting from the outer corner of the crease of the eye. Work toward the center of the eye following the natural crease of the eye and work it a little higher to create a shadow effect. Use the windshield washer method of blending (back and forth) and create a "V" in the outer corner of the eye. Working from the outer corner inward puts the majority of the color in that outer corner. If the intensity of color were in the inner corner it would make you look like someone gave you a black eye. See the correct application in the diagram below.

- Lighter shade (can use the medium shade for this also) is applied using the eye shadow brush. Blend from the inner corner of the eye upward under the eyebrow and blend with the darker shade so you can't tell where one color started and the other color finished.

Playing with Shiny Eye Shadow

While shiny eye shadows are fun and can create a sparkle for a younger, fun look, seasoned women should avoid any shiny or sparkle eye shadows or do what I do—mix those colors you like with a translucent face powder and apply. It cuts the shine, but keeps the color and you can have the best of both worlds.

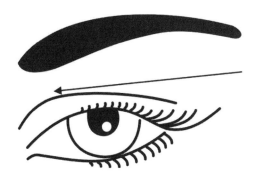

Eyeliner

This step is optional depending on whether you want your eyes to be larger or smaller, if your lid is larger or smaller, and what kind of effect you are seeking. Generally, most women look better with a thin line of darker color along the lash line that enhances the eyelashes and makes them look fuller and longer.

Use a darker color along the upper lashes: black, brown or dark blue. Black eyeliner on the upper lashes will make your lashes look longer and looks best with dark eyelashes and dark eyebrows. Brown eyeliner will make your lashes look fuller and works best on redheads and blonds with light colored eyelashes and eyebrows. Dark blue eyeliner works great on anyone and helps to bring out the whites of your eyes.

You can use a waterproof pencil, or to get the best look, use an eyeliner brush. Dampen the brush and apply a dark pigment eyeliner with featherlike strokes in and among the lashes. Follow the natural lash line. Don't worry about making a perfect line—use a cotton swab in a downward motion to clean up any imperfections in technique. Remember, practice makes perfect. You're sure to have this technique mastered in no time.

Use a lighter color under the bottom lashes, from the outer area of the eye into where the iris of the eye ends on the inside of the eye. Again a pencil can be used for this, or use your favorite color eye shadow and apply using an eyebrow brush. Remember, subtle is better. You don't want people to say "Wow—love that color under your eyes." You want them to say, "Wow, you look awesome today—what's different?"

Choosing an Eyeliner Color

Brown or hazel eyes look best with dark green eyeliner under the eye. It makes the eye "pop" and look alive. Blue eyes look best with dark blue eyeliner under the eye. It makes the eye look bright and brings out the whites of the eyes. Dark complexions look especially great using green or blue liner under the lower lashes as it really makes the eyes shine!

Use the Proper Tools

You will not be able to get the effect you would like for your eyes using a sponge applicator or inferior brushes. You must use the proper makeup tools to get the best effect. While Bobbi Brown® has great brushes—soft, usable and washable—Aloette has similar brushes at a fraction of the cost. Be sure to wash your brushes once a month with your hair shampoo and let them dry naturally standing up. This will make your brushes last longer.

Mascara

Black mascara makes your lashes look longer, brown makes them look thicker and blue under the eyes brings out the whites of your eyes. If you have the time, you can start by applying the brown, lengthening with the black and enhancing the lower lashes in blue. For most of us, time is an issue so stick with black or brown.

First, apply mascara on the upper part of your upper eyelashes in a downward motion. Then apply it on the bottom part of your upper lashes pulling the eyelashes upward and causing them to curl on their own. If this is not enough curl for you, use an eyelash curler on clean eyelashes before applying mascara.

On the lower lashes, mascara should be applied with the wand being held vertical and depositing color on the lower lashes and then brushed through with the wand held horizontally. Your outer lashes will always be the longest, so make the most of them and apply multiple coats of mascara to those areas.

Getting the Most From Your Eyelash Curler

You can "heat up" the eyelash curler by using your hair dryer for a few seconds to heat the metal and then curl your lashes. Be careful you don't get it too hot!

Choosing the Right type of Mascara

Stay away from using waterproof mascaras except on special occasions because the ingredients in them can be harmful to the eyes if used on a regular basis. My suggestion is to use a good mascara with the right brush. A good inexpensive mascara is Cover Girl® Lash Blast. On the more expensive end, consider Christian Dior® Show.

Eyebrows

You may not look at your eyebrows as a part of your makeup routine, but you should. The test is when you look at your face after application of all your makeup and something is missing. Most likely your eyebrows need darkening. Your eyebrows draw focus to your eyes. Improperly applied color to your eyebrows will make your eyes look unbalanced.

To see if you need this, simply apply a brown or grey or black color eye shadow with an eyebrow brush to your eyebrows—match your eyebrow color or hair. Start from the center of your eyebrow, work out to the end and then go back and apply the leftover color to the inner part of your eyebrows. This avoids too much color being applied on the inner portion of your eyebrow.

Deciding on the Length of Your Eyebrows

When you are younger, your eyebrows can be drawn down a little lower than the natural eyebrow line to give the appearance of larger eyes. The same goes for contour eye shadows being applied upward and outward to the outer corner of the eye. To determine where your line goes, use a pencil and place it from the outer corner of your mouth to the outer corner of your eye. Draw your eyebrows to this point. A more seasoned woman requires a shorter eyebrow and contour eye shadow line to give the appearance of a lifting of the eye. Using that same pencil, place it from the side of your nose to the corner of your eye and draw your eyebrows to this point.

Lip Liner

If you have a natural full lip, with a natural lip line, you won't need a lip liner. If you have no natural lip line—most of us don't—and don't know where to apply a lip liner, think, "connect the dots." Follow the natural line of your lip and dot the center of the lower outer lip, dot the lower outer corners of your mouth, draw an X on the bow of your mouth and a dot on the outer upper corners of your mouth. Play connect the dots, lining the upper lip from the inner corner out. Connect the dots on the lower lip from the outer corner and go in (see diagram). You will get so good at this you eventually won't even need a mirror. Use a color one shade darker than the lip color or lip shine you are wearing to create a definite mouth shape.

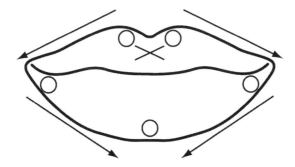

Choosing the Best Lip Liner Color for You

Be daring and try different colors. The best thing about using different lip liner colors is that you can use four different color lip liners and one lip color and get all sorts of different combinations because the lip liner changes the shade of the lip color and creates a new look every time. Pop in a couple different lip shine shades and you have an entire wardrobe of lips! It's great fun and sexy, too!

Lip Color

Lip color can be applied with a brush or straight from a tube—it's up to you. Look for a long-wearing color that has slip to it, meaning it slides easily onto the lips. You may pay a little more for a long-wearing lip color, but you will look good all the time and you won't constantly be reapplying your lipstick. Aloette has great long-wearing lipsticks and great colors from which to choose.

Share a gift of this book with someone who noticed a change in you and say, "*Image Power* did it for me—it can do it for you too!"

MOLLY KLIPP
Your Image Your Life
and Aloette Cosmetics of Seattle

(425) 280-9088
yourimageyourlife@comcast.net
www.yourimageyourlife.com
www.aloetteofseattle.com

Love of life, a keen and sincere interest in people and a desire to share her passion for helping others are the hallmark of Molly's life. She brings 26 years of experience in the image and glamour industry. Molly is a certified color analyst; makeup artist, and wardrobe planner helping you create your best look from everyday, business, to high glamour using her tools, skills and experience.

Molly moved to Seattle in 1985 knowing only one person in the State of Washington and started Aloette Cosmetics of Seattle. Since that time, through the law of attraction, Molly developed one of the top five organizations in the industry. Through talking to people everywhere, she has sold over $20 million in product and helped her sales force earn more than they ever dreamed. Molly has joyfully experienced life from stay-at-home mom to dynamic business leader and professional trainer and speaker.

Communicate with Class

Tips for the 21st Century

By Deborah King

People have been communicating since the beginning of time, but never has it been so challenging. Communication today embodies more than the written word or the familiar face-to-face interaction. We also communicate through cell phones, email, and text messaging. Knowing which medium to use, and using it with class, is no small feat.

Social events provide a captive audience for the individual who enjoys talking nonstop, rarely pausing long enough for you to say a word, while others cling to the food area hoping that if they continue eating, they will avoid the agony of speaking at all.

Cell phone users go about their daily business as though cocooned in their own personal cell phone booth. They leave others waiting for them while they fumble through their wallet to gather the funds for their purchase while chatting freely about the details of their evening plans.

Polishing your image requires you to give attention to your appearance, your behavior, and your communication skills. We all have encountered someone who looks fabulous, but behaves in an unruly manner or has irritating speech habits that negatively impact her credibility. It simply is not enough to select clothing appropriate for the situation that enhances your best features, and to execute your etiquette skills like a pro. You must also master your vocal delivery and refine your language so there is continuity in your overall message. This total package will provide a consistent message, empowering your image and announcing to all that you are a leader in your field.

Preparation is the Key to Successful Communication

Many believe that you were either born with the ability to be a good conversationalist, or you were not. This simply is not true. Good conversation does not just happen. You can master the needed skills to maneuver successfully through any social situation with ease. All it takes is preparation and practice.

So, how do you resist falling victim to the many communication blunders that can destroy your image and your relationships? How do you maintain class and style in today's fast-paced world? This rapidly changing landscape requires each of us to refine our verbal, nonverbal, and technological skills in order to communicate with class.

Vocal Delivery

Years ago, I attended an event where a beautifully dressed woman entered the room and caught my eye. Her movements were graceful, and her appearance was flawless. She captured the attention of all who saw her. Her magnetic pull drew me to her. I introduced myself and she replied with a nasal, high-pitched squeal, "Hello." I remember holding myself in check so I did not allow my face to reveal my shock. Here was a woman who had developed a beautiful sense of style and poise, but had neglected to also develop her voice so she was consistent in her personal message. This inconsistency erased all her other efforts.

Mastering a few details can greatly improve your vocal delivery. The first step is to analyze your voice. One way to do this is to tape record yourself while speaking in a casual manner with a friend. This setting tends to provide you with a good sample of your speech. As you listen to yourself, evaluate your tone, enunciation, articulation, volume, rate of speech, and use of language.

Vocal Tips

+ Develop a vocal tone that is in the mid–to-lower range. This level is more pleasant to the ear and will convey authority. Those with a high-pitched tone are seen as inexperienced and will not be taken seriously.

+ Practice fully enunciating your words.

+ End sentences with a vocal period. Women tend to end sentences with an upward inflection as though they are asking a question rather than making a statement. This pattern of speech makes you sound unsure and weak.

+ Speak at an appropriate level. Those who speak too softly are viewed as insecure or invisible; too loudly as brash and obnoxious.

+ Pace your speech so that you are interesting and easily understood. Women often speak too fast and rarely pause. Pausing demonstrates you are confident and comfortable and adds to your credibility.

+ Avoid using slang and vocal fillers. Words such as: 'like', 'um', 'kinda', 'sorta' and 'you know,' litter much of our communication today and diminish professionalism. Try replacing fillers with a pause.

+ Increase your vocabulary so you have a wider range of words from which to draw. I find that reading a variety of publications provides me with information to discuss with others, as well as increases my vocabulary.

Additional Conversational Tips

+ Allow others to finish their thought before making a comment. True class never interrupts or completes another person's story.

+ Avoid providing unsolicited advice. If they don't ask, don't tell! And, even if they do ask, make sure your feedback is appropriate and always kind.

+ Maintain a positive attitude. A person who is positive reflects poise and confidence.

+ Avoid the gossip pit; nothing tarnishes your image more quickly.

+ Only apologize when you truly mean to do so. Saying "I'm sorry" over and over again can become habitual and detract from your image.

+ Know when to quit talking. Due to nervousness, or wanting to press home a point, we can say far too much. Get to the point and then be silent.

+ Use the word 'and' instead of 'but' so you don't negate the other person. "I see what you mean, and I believe we can achieve your goals by . . ."

+ Respond to confrontational language by thanking the person for her thoughts and acknowledging her opinion. You do not have to agree with her to do this.

+ Match the other person's energy and emotion. We laugh with those who laugh and mourn with those who mourn.

+ Practice inviting signals, such as good posture, eye contact, a warm and sincere smile, and acknowledgement.

+ Practice good listening skills, such as nodding, making eye contact, and responding with interested comments to encourage them to continue speaking.

+ Master good posture: correct posture is not rigid, but upright and supports the body as it moves. The overall effect is one of effortless, graceful, assured movement.

+ Maintain a grateful and kind heart. Out of the abundance of your heart, your mouth speaks.

+ Be generous with "please," "thank you," "you are welcome," and "excuse me."

Eye Contact

Appropriate eye contact is vital for effective communication to take place. This includes consistent eye contact, limited blinking and focus. In our western culture, not making eye contact communicates a lack of confidence, a lack of interest, or deceit. A person who does not make eye contact is often seen as rude. Think of how you felt the last time you were talking with someone who constantly gazed around the room as though she was looking for someone better to come along. That person missed the opportunity to make you feel valued and demonstrate class.

On the other hand, to simply stare at someone will also make her feel very uncomfortable. Ten seconds of steady eye contact with little blinking, followed by a brief glance away, and then establish eye contact again, is a good pattern to follow.

How to Launch, Linger in, and Leave a Conversation

Launching a Conversation. Launching a conversation begins before you ever say a word. Your approach should include good posture, eye contact, and a sincere smile. This sets a positive and welcoming tone. Start your interaction with a greeting. If the person is new to you, you will want to introduce yourself. Your introduction should include a greeting, your name, and a firm handshake. If you already know the person, say hello and how nice it is to see them again.

If you would like to join others who are already in conversation, look for inviting signals. Two people facing each other who are intently focused on their conversation are not open to others. A group of three or more persons who have an opening in their circle would be inviting. This provides you with an open door to enter the conversation. Approach them with good posture and a warm smile, pause until the person is done speaking, then say hello and introduce yourself. By pausing, you will know the topic of conversation and easily be able to join in.

If you are visiting with others and you see someone would like to join you, it is a welcoming gesture to turn your body to include them, briefly make eye contact and smile. Once the person who is talking has completed her thought, acknowledge the newcomer with a greeting and direct the topic towards her.

Lingering in a Conversation. Many people do not know what to say following their initial greeting. Preparation for this moment will empower you with the confidence to proceed. Having a few questions you can ask the other person will help your conversation linger beyond hello. I encourage the youth I teach to start a question with one of the 5 W's they have learned in English: who, what, when, where, and why. A question that begins with one of these words will be an opened-ended question. Open-ended questions are best because they require more than a yes or no response, providing you with valuable feedback for further conversation.

Another great phrase that encourages conversation is to say, "Tell me about …" This lets the other person tell you whatever she may like about a given subject. For example, "Tell me about your family," will allow her to tell you about her children, spouse, parents, or, if she chooses, she can tell you about her cat and goldfish. People enjoy talking about their families, but asking a woman about her husband who, unknown to you, recently left her, would not be a wonderful way to start a conversation.

You can be viewed as a master conversationalist by simply asking people about themselves. A word of caution, though: simply asking a series of preplanned questions can make you come across as though you are a reporter. To be successful, you need to weave questions about the other person with information about yourself. Conversation requires two active participants.

Leaving a Conversation. Leaving a conversation takes as much finesse as launching and lingering. What do you do with the person who discovered you are so charming that she just doesn't want to leave? In most social gatherings, you will want to briefly talk with as many people as possible. Spending five to ten minutes per person is appropriate in these settings. If you are enjoying your conversation and realize there is not enough time during this interaction, set another appointment for lunch or coffee so you may pick up and continue.

It is important to use closing signals to indicate your conversation is coming to an end:

+ If you were sitting, stand.
+ Say how great it was to see them and you look forward to seeing them again.
+ Introduce them to another person.
+ Say you have enjoyed visiting with them and know others would also like to have some time with them.

+ Excuse yourself and say you have enjoyed visiting, but see another person you must connect with before the event is over.

Conversations often include something we said we would do: meet for lunch, send a photo, call them later or provide a service. If you have said you would follow up with something, make sure you do. No matter how small the commitment was, follow through and be a person of your word. This builds your credibility and provides people with a positive and professional view of you.

Consider writing a short handwritten note on nice paper to someone you just met, or to someone who has done something nice for you. These few short lines expressing how much you enjoyed meeting them, thanking them for their time, suggestion, or idea, will do more to improve your image than you can imagine. In a world of emails and text messaging, nothing beats the image power of a handwritten note.

Be a Good Listener

One of the greatest gifts we can give to another is a listening ear. Our fast-paced lifestyle has trimmed information into sound bites and thirty-second commercials. Taking the time to fully listen to someone communicates how much we value them.

Being a good listener does not mean you simply do not speak. Effective listening plays a vital and active role in communication.

Tips for Being a Good Listener

+ Practice good eye contact.
+ Suspend judgment.

+ Maintain a neutral position both verbally and nonverbally.

+ Allow the speaker to finish her thought completely before replying.

+ Avoid distractions.

+ Eliminate fidgeting.

+ Use prompts to encourage them to continue. This may be nodding your head, saying "uh-huh", or "that is interesting."

+ Restate her comments in your own words. This ensures you understood accurately and communicates you were listening.

Be Present in the Moment

Life is busier today than ever, and it is a real challenge to truly be focused on what someone is saying. Since we listen much faster than we speak, our mind is constantly trying to multi-task. As women, we fulfill many roles that require a great deal of energy. Mothers tell me how guilty they feel leaving their children so they can go to work, and then how guilty they feel at home because there is so much to do at work. Add to work the other roles we fulfill of being a wife, a friend, a volunteer, and managing our home, and it is no wonder we feel pulled in so many directions.

Make it a habit to practice being present in the moment. Notice the details, the smells, the cool breeze, warm sunshine, or refreshing rain. Hear not only your friend's words, but hear her heart. Don't let anything else steal this moment in time. Never again will you be in this place, with this person, engaged in this activity. You will never have a chance to dance this dance again.

Self-Talk

The most powerful conversation we have is with ourselves. Others may say all sorts of things about us, positive or negative, and we may or may not believe them. But, the words we speak about ourselves are the words that shape our self-image and direct our life. Here are some tips when speaking about yourself:

+ Speak honestly of your accomplishments.

+ Respond to a compliment with a simple and sincere thank you. When someone compliments you, never respond with all the things you think are wrong. In doing so, you are actually rejecting her compliment.

+ Surround yourself with positive people who build you up.

+ Take time daily to remind yourself of your positive qualities and that good things, wonderful people, and great opportunities are coming your way. Speak the things you desire, not the things you don't.

+ Speak of your future. You cannot change your past. Living in what could have been, or should have been, will only hold you prisoner to yesterday. Look out your windshield, not the rearview mirror!

Using Technology

Communication would not be complete without looking at how we present ourselves through technology. The benefit of using technology is speed. We are able to quickly communicate a thought or message without requiring much effort. The challenge is to properly identify the best method to convey your message and then do so appropriately. Most relationships will include a variety of communication methods.

Text messaging. This form of communication is best used for quick bits of information such as a time to meet or a quick question. It should be brief and to the point, much like writing a short note to someone.

Email. This is best used for communicating action items, facts, or, in social settings, friendly hellos:

- Email should never be used to communicate emotional or volatile information, such as ending a relationship or firing an employee.

- Your email name reflects your image and creates an impression about who you are. Select yours with care.

- Always read your email out loud prior to sending it. This allows you to check for errors and hear the tone of the message.

Carefully use social sites like Facebook and MySpace. It is common practice today for people to "Google" your name to gather information about you prior to entering into a professional relationship. Opportunities have been lost when a photo, taken in fun that was only meant to be shared with intimate friends, ended up online for all to see. Always ask yourself, would you want this photo, or this comment, played on the Five O'clock News? What is sent out into cyberspace lives forever!

Cell Phones. We can hardly imagine life today without them. They are an excellent way to quickly communicate information to others.

- In general, avoid doing another activity when you are speaking on your phone, especially in public. It is rude to expect a salesperson to assist you when you are not focused on them. Many stores have resorted to posting signs saying they will be happy to help you when you complete your call. Many states are now enacting laws making it illegal to use your phone while driving without a hands-free device.

+ Always ask the person you are calling if she is available to talk. Don't assume she is.

+ Place calls when you can be heard. Background noise and poor reception create frustration for the person on the other end of the call.

+ Be mindful of your image when selecting a ring tone. Novelty rings, although fun, do not convey professionalism. Your ring-tone volume should be set on low, or better yet, on vibrate or silent when with others.

+ Your hands-free earpiece should never be worn as a fashion accessory; it should only be worn when you are actually using your phone.

+ When leaving a message, state your full name and telephone number, slowly and clearly. We tend to hurry through this portion making it a challenge for the one being called to understand us.

+ Remember that whenever you use your mobile phone to text or talk in the presence of another person, you are telling them that something else is more important than she is. Make the person you are with your focus!

A wonderful as technology is, nothing replaces a face-to-face conversation for building relationships. Only in this interaction are you able to fully experience all the elements of communication and enjoy a full exchange of ideas and emotions. We may not remember the text message or email we received yesterday, but we will never forget lunch with a friend who heard our heart, shared our sorrows and joys, and empowered us to go out and face another day with grace and confidence.

The result of communicating well is that you are able to make the other person feel valued and honored. Communicating with class does not just happen, nor is it something you are born with. You can improve your communication skills and present a more polished image with preparation, practice and repetition. With focused effort, it will not be long before people will be commenting on how much they enjoy talking with you and how polished and poised you are.

DEBORAH KING
Final Touch Finishing School

Developing Skills for Life

(206) 510-5357
deborah@finaltouchschool.com
www.finaltouchschool.com

Deborah King is President of Final Touch Finishing School, Inc., which she founded in Seattle, Washington in 1989. At a young age, Deborah knew she wanted to help others project the best image possible. Her passion has always been to equip people from all walks of life with the necessary skills to be able to move confidently from informal to formal situations with ease and grace. She teaches her students how to evaluate the situation they are faced with and knowing what is appropriate for their dress and behavior.

Considered the Queen of Etiquette, Deborah's warm teaching style is based on the simplicity of kindness and respect for self, others and property. Her classes instill a greater sense of potential and increased confidence for all who attend.

Deborah is a certified etiquette and image consultant, an active member of the Association of Image Consultants International, the National Speakers Association, and an affiliate with the Conselle Institute of Image Management. She travels extensively throughout the United States and internationally, teaching her principles of etiquette and poise to individuals from five to seventy-five.

Etiquette Is Not Dead

Refining Your Skills for Greater Confidence and Success

By Marion Gellatly, AICI CIM

It's A Package

Contrary to what you may think, your image is not just about appearance. Appearance plays a significant role, but there's more to the package—and that includes how you treat people and make others feel when they're with you. It includes your personal conduct and how you project yourself in every situation. It's the energy you bring into a room, how you greet others, shake hands, make introductions, and entertain or dine together. All of these skills require well-honed etiquette finesse and will build your powerful presence in business or in your social life.

At some time in your professional life, you've probably experienced an awkward moment or two. While dining with a client or attending a social event, maybe you found yourself unsure which bread plate is yours, so you avoid reaching for a roll. Maybe you found yourself drinking from the wrong coffee cup and the person next to you is left wondering which cup is hers. Maybe you fumbled over a crucial business introduction—you ended up winging it and regretted the outcome. Maybe you hugged a client instead of shaking his hand, felt him stiffen, and wondered if you offended him. Worse yet, maybe you found yourself without your business card at an unexpected but critical meeting with someone you've wanted to meet for a long time. Finding yourself in any of these situations is bound to shake your confidence and might raise a question or two in the minds of others. You can't afford this in today's competitive business world.

In over 15 years of image and etiquette coaching, I've discovered that my clients have common worries about their behavior: what's appropriate, what's accepted and what isn't—things that are not often learned at home or in school. I remind them that etiquette is not about being perfect or pretentious, but it is about looking polished and feeling confident and comfortable with anyone in any social or business situation.

Demonstrating Your Etiquette Skills Will Open Doors That Money and Position Cannot

As a savvy woman, it's critical to observe, learn, refine, and practice your etiquette skills. Guaranteed to distinguish you in today's business world, these key strategies and practices will boost your confidence, produce great results, and outclass your competition.

Set the Tone with a Confident Handshake

How you shake hands can speak louder than your words. An important symbol of respect, a solid handshake communicates self-confidence. Unfortunately, it is often overlooked by women. Make it routine, and follow these steps for a confident execution:

+ Always stand up, unless for some reason it's impossible. It demonstrates your respect.

- Have good posture with shoulders parallel and your weight evenly distributed on both feet. It demonstrates your confidence.

- Look the person in the eye and maintain eye contact. It lets her know she is most important to you at this moment.

- Extend your right hand in a vertical position with your thumb up and out. It positions your hand for a good connection.

- Engage a web-to-web grip and shake from the elbow, not from the shoulder or wrist. It keeps the greeting controlled.

- Shake easy and gentle with a firm touch; no bone crusher, limp wrist, double clasp (except when expressing sympathy) or six-shake handshakes. No hugs or kisses in business, as they can be misinterpreted as an invasion of a person's personal space and are an embarrassing interaction to some. It keeps everyone comfortable. In a social situation, use your judgment before deciding to hug or kiss. Will it make the other person feel awkward or uncomfortable? This is key to your decision.

- Smile and introduce yourself with a confident voice, using your first and last name. It shows your warmth and openness.

- Give 2–3 smooth shakes and then let go. It's simple and complete.

Handshakes belong just about anywhere you meet a business associate, even outside a business setting, such as shopping malls or grocery stores. Make it a common practice to convey your respect for others by offering a confident handshake, even in social settings.

Introduce with Intention

Right behind a confident handshake comes a skillful introduction. Have you ever found yourself standing among a group of people and no one introduces you? Does it make you feel invisible and uncomfortable? Maybe they've forgotten your name, and don't want to let on. Always help when you notice they don't recall your name or are having trouble with the pronunciation.

Even if you're not the official host, behave like one and start introductions if no one takes the lead. The most important thing for you to remember about introductions is to make them, even if you forget someone's name. Studies have found people would rather you ask their name, than not be introduced at all.

If you're entertaining a client and wish to introduce her to one of your business associates, always remember the client is the most important individual in business hierarchy. Therefore, the client's full name is always said first and your associates are introduced to her. For example, "Mary Peterson (client), I would like to introduce to you the General Manager of our hotel, Susan Smith. Susan, Mary has recently booked her company's conference with our hotel." When appropriate, try to mention something of mutual interest, for example: "Mary, I understand you and Susan are both marathon runners." This gives the parties the opportunity to talk about something they have in common and brings familiarity to them. It also demonstrates your courtesy and concern for their comfort.

In social settings, the formula for introductions is slightly different. As with business, you always say the name of the most important person first. In business, the order of importance regardless of gender is: first the client, then the most senior executive, followed by junior executive, and so forth down the line. In social settings, the order of importance does consider gender; for example, first the senior woman, followed by senior man, then junior woman, followed by junior man. An example of a social introduction is, "Sue Smith (senior woman), this is my neighbor, Peter Jones (senior or junior man). Peter, Sue is a friend from church and was the first person I met when I moved here."

Exchange Your Identity

Always carry clean, fresh and accessible business cards as they communicate your identity—professional or personal. They're important whether you're in business, are retired, are a volunteer in your community, or in a job transition. Your card should give your contact information, including your email address and web site, if you have one.

As a woman, I'm sure you change purses frequently, and in your haste, may forget to transfer your business cards. You can't afford to get caught without them, especially when a potential client you've been hoping to do business with asks for your card. It's an embarrassment for you, and making an excuse doesn't start the relationship well. The simple solution is to buy several quality card cases—leather or metal—fill them with your business cards and slip one into every purse, briefcase, and car. That way, you're guaranteed to have them when and where you need them. The case also protects your cards and keeps them in excellent condition representing your image. Pulling your card from a case is more professional than digging in the bottom of your purse. Also, be sure to give and receive business cards respectfully (use both hands with Asian cultures), with the printing facing the person receiving your card. When receiving a card, take a moment to look at it before putting it away. This demonstrates respect for those you meet.

Prepare to Dine with Class

More business in America is conducted over restaurant tables than in offices. We take clients to breakfast, lunch, tea, cocktails, and dinner to discuss business and strengthen relationships. Prospective employees are often evaluated over a meal, as are current employees in line for a promotion. As our lives get busier, we are socializing with friends more frequently outside the home. Therefore, your social etiquette skills can often be a determining factor in your success with clients, superiors and colleagues.

It's a fact that many of today's business people were reared on microwave meals or spent evenings in the drive-thru lane of a fast-food establishment. Neither fostered the etiquette skills required to dine with polish in today's business world.

It was a recent evening in the California wine country when my husband and I were dining in a quaint, well-known restaurant. The setting was lovely, the service impeccable, and every table in the intimate dining room was full. Next to us was a well-dressed, thirty-something-year-old couple. It appeared they were enjoying a business dinner rather than a dinner date. As the dinner service started, I couldn't help but notice the etiquette skills of the young woman. At first, I gave her the benefit of the doubt. She must be so focused on the conversation that she's not paying attention to what she's doing, I justified. But I quickly came to understand I was giving her far too much credit. First, the appetizer arrived and her napkin remained on the table. As she started to eat, she grabbed the fork in her fist like a construction worker might, and began shoveling. It continued like this throughout the dinner service—one faux pas after another. What must the gentleman be thinking, I wondered? He surely noticed!

You get the picture, and have probably witnessed a similar scenario yourself. Did the gentleman choose to overlook the crass behavior of his dining partner? Was he feeling uncomfortable with her manners? One thing I knew for certain: if this woman was interviewing for a job or entertaining a client, the deal was "off" by the first course! You aren't born with dining skills, but it's a necessity to learn them for business and social interactions today.

Here are some failsafe tips for entertaining and dining that will guarantee a positive memory of you in the eyes of your clients, superiors, colleagues or anyone with whom you want to make a great impression.

Implement Your Dining Strategy

To be a successful host in today's world, there are many things to consider before you ever get to the restaurant. It's your responsibility to see that your guests have a great dining experience with you. It begins with your invitation and restaurant selection.

Be clear in your invitation. When you invite someone to dine with you, make it clear you will be the host and will be paying. For example, "I'd like you to be my guest for lunch next week to thank you for your business." Then suggest several restaurant options and let your guest choose. Always make reservations. If the restaurant doesn't accept reservations, don't offer that restaurant as an option.

Developing relationships with key restaurants is important to ensure a smooth dining experience. By frequenting a few excellent restaurants regularly, you'll understand the food preparation and be able to make confident recommendations to your guest. Get acquainted with the manager and servers so you'll receive great service and have special requests honored.

Call your guest the day before to confirm the time and place and provide them with the restaurant's address. Then reconfirm with the restaurant to avoid any slip-ups. Exchange cell phone numbers with your guest in case there is a delay or something unforeseen occurs.

If you are on a budget I recommend that you meet at 10:00 a.m. for coffee, between 2:00-4:00 p.m. for tea, or at 7:00 p.m. for coffee and dessert. If you consistently go to the same locations, you'll receive great service and not be rushed as long as you leave a good tip.

Arrive in advance. Arrive 10 minutes ahead of your reservation and ask to have your table pointed out. This gives you the opportunity to make any changes if necessary. Always avoid tables in high traffic or noisy areas. A quiet table is always the best for conversation. Take your server aside and explain the bill should come to you, or let him take a credit card imprint right then. Wait for your guest in the lobby. Let her precede you as you walk to the table. You can guide your guest to the seat with the best view, and she should be seated first.

Be strategic about ordering. Offer recommendations to your guest. It lets your guest know what is good and also gives her a clue about an appropriate price range. Invite your guest to order first for strategic reasons. That way you'll be able to match your order to the courses of food that your guest orders. If she orders a salad, then you order soup, salad or appetizer to accompany her. The main objective is to ensure that your guest is not left to eat alone.

Make sure what you order is easy to eat so you're able to carry on a conversation. Do not order anything messy, crunchy or that you must eat with your hands. Choose simple knife-and-fork foods. Remember the goal of the meal is to get to know each other better and strengthen the relationship, not struggle with your meal.

Use your napkin wisely. The napkin is primarily used to protect your clothing although it is also used for blotting your mouth. This doesn't mean wiping off your lipstick before the meal. Use a tissue to blot your lipstick prior to sitting down at the table to prevent leaving a lipstick mark on the napkin or on the rims of glasses. Place your napkin in your lap when everyone is seated, not before. If the napkin is large, fold it in half with the fold toward you and the open end toward your knees. This way if you get something messy on your fingers you can simply wipe them between the folds. If you must get up from the table during the meal, place your napkin on the arm or seat of the chair, never on the tabletop. When you leave at the end of the meal, this is the time to loosely fold it and put it at your place setting. Never crumple it and put it on food or a soiled plate.

Elbows on the table are okay if there is no food being served or eaten. Wrists and forearms positioned on the edge of the table are always preferred throughout the meal rather than placing them in your lap.

Learn the proper place settings and utensils. Have you ever been unsure which bread plate is yours, especially at a round table? Or which fork is used for the salad versus the entree? Are your water and wine glasses on the right or left of your place setting? Simple etiquette wisdom says:

Solids to the left, liquids to the right. This means your bread plate will be to the left and your water, wine and coffee will be to the right of your place setting. Think of the BMW acronym: Bread on the left, Meal in the middle, Water on the right. Of the glassware, the water glass is typically closest to you. The other stemware is usually brought to you as needed and placed to the right of the water glass.

Utensils should be used starting from the outside and moving toward the dinner plate, which means the salad fork will be farthest to the left and the dinner fork to the right of the salad fork. If you aren't having a salad, your server should remove the salad fork for you.

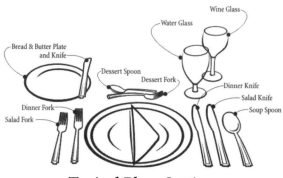

Typical Place Setting

Be conscious about drinking. Ask your guest what she would like and then follow her lead. If she orders alcohol, you can too, but limit your drink to one light one for lunch; and at most, two for dinner. If she doesn't drink, you don't drink. If you don't drink, order a non-alcoholic beverage. Whatever you choose, order with confidence. Be sure not to make excuses for ordering the drink of your choice.

Make a great toast. As a very important part of entertaining, we toast to honor, thank, and congratulate each other, to celebrate relationships and successes. If you are the host and wish to give a welcoming toast to a group of guests, stand and offer it as soon as all guests have been served their beverage. Don't tap your glass with a knife to get everyone's attention. Simply stand and this will draw attention to your impending toast. In a very small group, you should stay seated. When offering a toast, look at the person being toasted and offer your words. When you are done, raise your glass and drink. Then nod and put your glass down on the table. If you are the one being toasted, never drink to yourself. Simply nod, smile your appreciation for the honor, or say a few words of thanks.

Be sure to watch your host and follow her lead before you immediately grab your glass and start drinking. If no toast is forthcoming and your host starts drinking from her glass, you can follow suit.

Wait to begin the business discussion. For breakfast or lunch, let at least 10 minutes lapse before business is discussed, and for dinner the earliest business conversation can begin after the orders have been taken. This gives you the opportunity to enjoy your guest's company and get to know them on a more personal level before business discussions. Never put your briefcase, cell phone, PDA, purse, or keys on the tabletop. Documents are okay if needed during a business discussion. Laptops are being seen more at restaurants. If you need one for your discussion, wait until the meal is finished, and change seats to get closer to your guest. Turn your cell phone and beeper off or to "vibrate." No exceptions!

Minimize problems. If you have an issue with the food or service, discuss it with the restaurant manager away from your guest. You do not want to create an uncomfortable situation for the guest.

End the meal on a high note. Always conclude your business meal with a statement of how much you enjoyed time with your guest. For example: "Thank you for joining me for lunch today. I appreciate your business and the opportunity to work together. It's been a pleasure to get to know you better. We'll do this again."

Be a gracious guest. You have responsibilities to help make the experience a success, too. Begin by arriving at the restaurant on time; and if there's a delay, call your host's cell phone to let her know your arrival time. Be sure to ask if this will cause any problem.

If you have any food concerns and your host doesn't ask about them, let her know that you're a vegetarian. You want to avoid her embarrassment if she plans to take you to a steak house. If an issue arises with your meal, you can handle it discreetly yourself; or, if it's a major problem, bring it to your host's attention and have her deal directly with the service staff.

Being prepared for good conversation is another responsibility as a guest. What's happening in the community, in local news, the sports world, the company, the business world—any of these topics can offer stimulating conversation. But stay away from politics, religion, or anything that offers controversy.

Remember that a phone call, an email, or a written note of thanks will be appreciated by your host, and it conveys your courtesy and professionalism. It's sometimes the little things that count most.

Practice Makes Perfect

Now it's time to assess the quality of your etiquette skills and strategies for building and maintaining solid relationships with other people. What areas need your immediate attention?

- If it's a greeting and handshake, practice with your friends and family and ask for their feedback. Is yours too strong and overpowering, too gentle and wimpy, or just right? Keep trying until you get it right.

- If it's introductions, begin today by making them. That's most important. Assess who is the most important person in the scenario, and say that person's name first. Then, introduce others to that person. Offer each party a little information about the other, such as their relationship to you and a common interest. Be sure to review the differences between business and social introductions. The more you make introductions, the more confident you'll become.

- If it's forgetting your business cards, go now and buy several card cases. Strategically place them in every purse, briefcase, portfolio, and car that you use for business. Don't leave home without them.

- If it's your dining skills, take a friend or your significant other to dinner and practice in their company what you've learned today. One time play the host, and the next time play the guest. Make a note of the things you're still unsure of and try again.

When mastered, all of these skills will distinguish you as a confident, savvy professional whose business and social relationships are built on preparation, respect, and a genuine caring for others—a small investment that will pay big dividends in life.

MARION GELLATLY, AICI CIM
Powerful Presence^{SM}

Image management for today's world.

(831) 625-2000
info@powerful-presence.com
www.powerful-presence.com

Marion Gellatly is an internationally recognized leader in the field of image development. She is the founder and driving force behind *Powerful Presence*, her California-based image management training and consulting firm. Marion helps her clients find their full potential by improving their personal presentation through appearance, belief in self, positive attitude, communication, and business etiquette skills.

She travels extensively across the U.S. as a speaker and seminar leader, and is often called upon to serve as a media spokesperson on radio on the subjects of image and etiquette. Marion's clients feel that her insights are profound. Her advice is clear, concise and practical, and helps her clients present an image that is a living message of success.

Marion has been featured in national media such as *The New York Times, The Wall Street Journal* and *USA Today*. She is the author of *Your Powerful Presence: 125 Ways to Amplify Your Professional Image*. Marion is one of a handful of individuals who have earned the title, Certified Image Master, from the Association of Image Consultants International. She was AICI's 2005–2007 International President. AICI educates, supports and promotes image professionals in over 47 countries worldwide.

Unleash your Career with Business Casual Style

How to Become More Influential by Dressing Powerfully for Every Business Occasion

By Sarah Hathorn, AICI CIP

When dressing for work, women today have many choices—perhaps too many! Let's face it. Mastering our personal image is easier than dressing for our career. After all there are fashion magazines and blogs and even TV shows all showing us how to look great outside of our 9-5 work day. Although every woman wants to look stylish, professional and powerful when doing business, we face a greater challenge than men do because we have so many more wardrobe options.

When your clothing is out of sync with a business occasion, it hurts your chances with clients and colleagues. If you're like most professional women, on at least one occasion you've felt confident in a business casual outfit—until you get to the event and find you're underdressed. This makes it hard to fit in and communicate comfortably. You might feel awkward and certainly not at your best.

To feel confident in any business situation, you must master the four levels of business casual options. Then as situations arise, you will automatically choose the appropriate level of business casual dress. Your wardrobe will then help you make the right impression. You will:

+ Feel more confident and have higher self-esteem.

+ Make stronger connections and have more influence over those you meet.

+ Experience greater business success.

+ Attract many more opportunities in both the personal and professional areas of your life.

Whether you want to climb the corporate ladder to a high-level executive position, or simply grow your business by attracting more clients, projecting a savvy business casual image will help you achieve greater career success.

Your Visual Image Makes or Breaks Your First Impression

People make judgments seconds after meeting you, and your visual image plays a decisive role in shaping their opinions.

According to psychologist Albert Mehrabian, your appearance and body language account for 55 percent of the impression you make. Your voice accounts for 38 percent and the words you use only 7 percent.

So you must be aware that how you dress sends silent messages. Your wardrobe tells the world who you are and who you wish to become. It communicates your life goals, dreams and aspirations. It expresses the way you feel about yourself inside—at least that's what the people you meet are going to assume.

Making the best impression you can is critical because you're constantly competing with colleagues whose education and skill level are similar to yours.

Your polished business casual image can be the one competitive edge you have in making a customer feel more comfortable with you than with one of your peers. So it's worth the effort to maintain a consistently polished image.

Image Was Easy with Premier Dress

For decades, professionals typically wore what I call Premier Dress—the traditional business wardrobe that includes a coordinated, skirted business suit worn with hosiery and leather pumps. Financial professionals wear it almost every day so that they appear conservative and trustworthy. Although Premier Dress may seem a little stuffy, it is easy to recognize and master.

The bewildering options arrived in the late 1980s when powerful technology company executives started wearing what we now call Business Casual and the style took hold. At that time I was working at Macy's, Inc., as a store manager. When Macy's announced that all our stores across the country would be moving to the new business casual dress, confusion and havoc ensued. We were the world's largest department store, well known for helping women select fashionable wardrobes, and yet we could not define what this new phenomenon was.

I had to learn quickly about the new business casual attire, and since then have kept up with its improvements. Today it is defined as a casual version of business dress. Here's a quick shortcut: think of "business" first and "casual" second. When you put business first, you'll always go with a more refined business casual look and avoid the temptations of inappropriate weekend wear.

However, to consistently present a professional image, you need more than a few quick tips. You must master the four levels of business casual that fall between Premier Dress and weekend wear:

+ Refined Casual
+ Essential Casual
+ Evening Refined Casual
+ Informal Casual

Refined Casual: The New Norm for Business

Although one notch down from Premier Dress, Refined Casual is a sophisticated, professional look that gives great attention to detail.

It almost always involves a jacket—the most powerful item in your wardrobe. But because this style lets you mix and match your jacket with other core pieces, it conveys "casual" while maintaining your power and professionalism.

When to Wear It

Wear Refined Casual when you are representing your company or your own business and want to project a commanding visual presence.

For example, you'd wear this level when meeting with a potential client or current customer, speaking at an event, in the presence of high-level executives, or interviewing for a position where you would do any of these things.

Top-level executives in large companies serving conservative fields such as banking, accounting and finance, government, politics, law, and television tend to dress in this fashion when they're not wearing Premier Dress. Those working in highly creative fields like retail, advertising, marketing, publishing, and the entertainment industry tend to wear this level with a bit more fashion flair.

If you're an independent business professional or entrepreneur, I advise you to make Refined Casual your workday norm. Be sure to wear it if it is your employer's norm. Organizations want their people to represent their company's brand in a positive light. The image a company spends so much money to convey in their marketing can be dashed when a client or prospect meets an employee whose personal image does not align with the company brand.

Companies who recognize that their people send their strongest marketing messages often invest in their employees' personal image. One large international firm hired me to coach a few recently promoted female executives whose new responsibilities included speaking internationally and representing the organization across the globe. While they felt these women were extremely intelligent and had great speaking skills, their appearance did not align with the professional image of the company's brand. I helped these women master Refined Casual and they immediately saw results. They experienced more respect from clients and colleagues, and were even called upon to mentor and lead others as positive role models. Today,

Refined Casual keeps those women on the fast track of that organization.

The Image Message Refined Casual Conveys

By some measures, Refined Casual is the most important style for you to master because it helps you convey an image that is influential, credible and powerful.

Professionals prefer this style because a jacket communicates that you are a leader and an authority in the type of work you do. When you wear a jacket, people perceive that they can trust you, and view you as a true professional.

When I coach individuals like attorneys, CPAs, financial advisors, or salespeople—anyone in a profession where clients place a great deal of trust in them—I always recommend wearing a jacket because it sends a silent message of integrity and respect.

How to Put It Together

You'll need these essentials in your wardrobe to master the Refined Casual look:

+ **Tops:** tailored blouses, feminine dressy blouses, fine-gauge knit shells, sweaters and vests

+ **Bottoms:** Dress slacks, tailored work skirts, wrinkle-free khakis

+ **Dresses:** Tailored dresses in dark or neutral solid colors, preferably worn with a jacket

+ **Suits:** Coordinated pantsuits with traditional or modern jackets

The key to pulling off this look is to mix and match your separate core pieces and wear a jacket. To pull off this look quickly and easily every morning, it's essential to own a variety of great jackets.

Here are some guidelines for building your Refined Casual wardrobe:

+ Invest in a dark, neutral color suit that includes a jacket, skirt and pants, and then add coordinating blouses, pants and skirts. By mixing and matching these core pieces, you can create between 12 and 15 different outfits.

+ Choose core pieces with high-quality fabrics and classic styling. You'll get longer wear and greater versatility for your investment.

+ Take your core pieces to a fabulous tailor for a little nip and tuck so they fit you perfectly. You'll get that elegant look that emphasizes your credibility and expertise.

Remember that you get what you pay for. You'll look your absolute best in higher quality items that drape better over your silhouette.

If you're meeting with a client and feel overdressed in Refined Casual, the solution is easy: simply remove your jacket to convert your look to essential casual and your client will feel more at ease.

Essential Casual: Getting the Work Done

Like Refined Casual, Essential Casual is a sophisticated look that requires attention to detail. However, because it does not include a jacket, it works best in a shirtsleeve, "get it done" operational environment.

The defining look at this level is a great tailored shirt or a dressy blouse. Choose a collared shirt whenever possible because it's more authoritative and powerful. You may be able to wear a polo shirt with a collar, but only if it stays crisp, maintains its shape and looks business-like.

When to Wear It

Wear essential casual when you work with the same people day after day or when you work alone.

For example, you'd wear this level if you work in a back office and don't see outside clients, or if you're a consultant or coach and work in the privacy of your own home. Some companies may adapt this level of dress in their more casual work environments. For example, many banks have adopted Essential Casual as the standard for their tellers.

The Image Message Essential Casual Conveys

This level is tricky to master because if it does not match your job responsibilities and career aspirations, it can send the wrong message and limit your advancement.

Unfortunately, women are perceived differently than men when they dress casually. Casual clothing tempts people to misjudge your credibility and status. If you dress too casually, you may be perceived as holding a job that's actually beneath yours on the corporate ladder.

Essential Casual can help you be comfortable while getting operational work done either by yourself or with well-known colleagues. However, it is not appropriate when your focus is on representing your business or building relationships.

Remember that leaders are *always* building relationships. So if you want to be a leader, or if your job includes influencing employees, prospects or clients, or if you want to advance in your career and do any of these things, I would advise you to dress in Refined Casual and convey the most powerful, influential image you can.

Dressing for the job you want can have a powerful effect on your career. For example, an attorney client of mine was up for promotion to become a partner in her firm. She had always dressed in the Essential Casual style, but I explained to her that in order to achieve a more commanding presence, she needed to incorporate Refined Casual into her working wardrobe. After several months of transitioning her image and wardrobe, she became one of the few partners appointed to her firm that year.

How to Put It Together

Discover some fashionable, classic-trend essentials to create your unique style in this tier:

- **Tops:** Dressy blouses, sweaters, vests, cardigan-shell twin sets, fine-gauge knit blouses, tailored shirts, polo shirts, company logo shirts
- **Bottoms:** Dress trousers, dressy casual skirts, wrinkle-free khakis
- **Dresses:** Dressy, more casual dresses

Many women take the easy, comfortable route and adopt the khakis-and-polo-shirt look as their work uniform, but they're missing the great potential at this level.

The key to making this look work in your favor is to pair a great modern top with stylish trousers or a dressy casual skirt— a professional-length skirt made of quality fabric. Have fun finding tops that fit and flatter you. Here are some suggestions for building your Essential Casual wardrobe.

+ Experiment with dresses and skirts. When shopping with a client, I always bring a surprise item to the fitting room: a skirt or dress. We're both delighted when she sees how feminine and powerful she can look when not always dressing like a man.

+ If you have shapely lower legs, show them off. When you show your lower leg, you are highlighting a more slender area of your body and creating a more slender silhouette. What woman doesn't want to look more slender?

+ Add a third piece to your outfit. Top off your trousers with a tailored blouse and a cardigan sweater to look more stylish and comfortable. When you add a third piece like a sweater or vest, it's amazing how much more polished you look.

+ Invest in high-quality core pieces. You can quickly be perceived as too casual or sloppy if your clothes are not tailored, do not drape properly, or are too loose or too tight. Be sure your appearance is business-like and does not lean towards weekend wear.

Evening Refined Casual:
Mixing Business with Pleasure

This level adds a bit of glitz and drama to the Refined Casual style. Jackets and shirts are dressier with more elegant fabrics and finer detailing. Sweaters and blouses can be embellished with pearls, beads or metallic threads. As a result, Evening

Refined Casual entails more allure, which can be powerful if you don't overdo.

When to Wear It

Evening Refined Casual is a great look when you're attending an evening dinner with colleagues, a cocktail party with prospects, or a special occasion at a client's place of business. It also works when you're entertaining a business client over dinner or participating in an evening networking function.

The Image Message
Evening Refined Casual Conveys

This level of dress is a casual elegant evening style that is perfect for after-hours business meetings. The Evening Refined Casual look is sophisticated and conveys you are detail-oriented, dignified and dressed appropriately for a special business occasion.

How to Put It Together

When you're shopping for Evening Refined Casual, look for these essentials. Remember black or rich jewel tones are always appropriate at this level, regardless of the season.

- **Tops:** Silk blouses, embellished or silk camisoles, beaded sweaters, pashminas or dressy evening wraps
- **Bottoms:** Silk pants, black dressy skirts, black dress slacks
- **Dresses:** Little black dresses, feminine flirty print dresses
- **Suits:** Dressy suits and evening jackets made of silk or other fine fabrics

- ✦ **Accessories:** Pearls, fine jewelry or chandelier earrings, strappy evening sandals, stiletto's, small clutch

Be prepared to dress up your daytime Refined Casual outfit when you know you'll be socializing with executives, clients or prospects immediately after work. If you have a professional evening event coming up on your calendar, figure out a way to remind yourself of it in the morning so you can wear something by day that's easy to change quickly for evening.

For example, in the morning you might put on a little black dress with a blazer for work and pack some enhancements for evening. Then after work on your way to the event you could remove the jacket, switch to black beaded chandelier earrings, add a dramatic necklace, slip on your strappy black sandals, throw the pashmina around your shoulders, grab your black evening clutch and voilá! You've got evening allure.

Informal Casual: Taking a Break from the Office

This level lets you dress comfortably for long-term outings in public environments. It features softer fabrics in more comfortable cuts so you can move more easily or stay cool in warm climates.

Your personal comfort, however, is not the main feature of the Informal Casual style. Its purpose is to help you look professional in environments where you're going to encounter prospects, clients or colleagues as well as the public.

When to Wear It

Wear the Informal Casual style when you're traveling to an annual conference or company retreat at a resort or other casual environment. If you're building a business that depends on recruiting local clients, wear this to the grocery store. You might also wear this look when you are entertaining a client at a sporting event.

The Image Message Informal Casual Conveys

This level sends the message that you are easy-going and approachable. Remember you are still representing your company while traveling, running errands, or attending an informal event. Although you may wear something a bit more informal, be sure you look stylish and professional.

How to Put It Together

Seek out these great essentials to wear to a conference, retreat or other work-related event:

- **Tops:** More casual style shirts, modern cardigan to wear over sundress
- **Bottoms:** Capri pants, casual skirts, khakis
- **Dresses:** Sheath dresses, sundresses, or knit jersey separates
- **Colors:** Bright, bold colors, or pastel colors—something that contrasts with the business-appropriate dark neutrals you normally wear
- **Prints:** Bolder prints like Hawaiian, floral or geometric that can be distracting at the office
- **Accessories:** Casual style shoes like sandals, flats, or wedges

Follow these guidelines when putting together your informal casual look:

+ Shop for finer resort wear. Look for core pieces at Lilly Pulitzer, Tommy Bahama, Chico's and J. Jill. Some department stores' private labels, such as Macy's INC® line, also work well at this level.

+ Look for wrinkle-free knits. When you're traveling, knits from Chico's are ideal. They'll keep you comfortable on a long flight and looking freshly pressed and professional when you check into the resort.

+ Guard against weekend wear. Avoid anything that's too baggy or too tight, too bulky or too transparent, or too youthful or too revealing. And when you get back to work, remember your informal clothes are too casual for office attire.

Start Mastering Your Business Casual Image Today

Investing in a Business Casual wardrobe is one of the best things you can do to become more successful in your professional life.

When I shop with my clients, I inspire them to understand how these dressing tools are similar to the law of attraction. Simply by looking stylish, professional and polished, you attract more elite clients and prestigious jobs.

When you wear a wardrobe that suits your style—one that reflects your personal brand of who you are and who you want to be, and is appropriate for your professional lifestyle—you feel at ease and can focus on your work productivity and career path. That's important because your image goes with you everywhere 24/7.

Everyone you meet is forming opinions about you. Get started now and make sure your first impressions are all good ones.

From Invisible to Influential

When you implement these Business Casual strategies, you will begin to form your signature style, which will reflect and express your personal brand and what you want out of your life. People will see you differently and new business opportunities will magically appear. It's exciting when it all comes together because when you look your absolute best, you feel ready to conquer the world. You experience an internal shift and gain greater confidence.

Most important, you'll move from invisible to influential. With a polished presence I guarantee you will see many more doors of opportunity open for you in your personal and professional lives. I hope you will use these dressing tools and experience the image journey that will bring your goals and dreams into reality.

SARAH HATHORN, AICI CIP
Illustra Image Consulting

Perception is Reality

(678) 528-1239
sarah@illustraimageconsulting.com
www.illustraimageconsulting.com

Sarah Hathorn began her fashion career over 20 years ago with Macy's, Inc. While there she served as a divisional vice president and general manager. She possesses a realistic view of the ever-changing corporate environment and understands its professional challenges.

As president and owner of Illustra Image Consulting in Atlanta, Georgia, Sarah helps her clients develop a more polished image resulting in greater self-confidence so they can achieve their professional and personal goals. Sarah also provides training seminars geared especially for professional services companies wishing to improve their brand image and positioning within the marketplace.

Sarah is internationally trained as a certified image consultant through the London Image Institute, a premier global training organization. She also received training in color theory and principles through the Sci-Art Company. She currently serves as president on the Executive Committee of the Atlanta Chapter of the Association of Image Consultants International (AICI), the most prestigious trade association in the worldwide image industry. Sarah has been featured in *New You Magazine* and is a co-author of the e-book entitled, How to Look Stylish. She is a frequent radio show co-host and guest.

Short and Chic

Using the Magic of Illusion to Look Taller and More Stylish

By Kimberly Law, AICI CIP

For those of us under 5'4", assembling a wardrobe can be a nightmare. A typical scenario might go like this: You put off shopping for as long as you can, then finally desperation forces you out to the stores. While walking down the street or through the mall, you bypass most of the boutiques—not because you don't love the clothes or have no desire to dress fashionably, but because you know that finding something that fits or even comes close to fitting is very unlikely. You know from experience that even in a department store you will be limited to the "Petite" department, which is indeed, petite. As you browse the racks, your heart sinks further because the manufacturers got it wrong, yet again. No, we petites are not all the same age and not all the same shape. Not all of us want to look like teenagers, little girls or the sweet grandmotherly type either. Some of us want to appear stylish, chic and yes—taller.

As you can probably tell, I feel your frustration. I'm 5'3" myself and have experienced all those shopping disappointments and more. But there is hope. Although it seems you have few options to choose from and the few you do find are all wrong, you can find ways to be short and still appear chic by applying the magic of focal points, scale, line, and fit.

Focal Points: Putting First Things First

The first thing you need to determine is where do you want people to look? Whatever stands out the most, attracts the most attention and creates a focal point. For instance, if you wear bright red shoes with an otherwise neutral outfit, the eye will be drawn to the shoes. If you wear a neutral outfit, neutral shoes and a bright colored scarf, the scarf creates the focal point and attracts attention. Here's the trick: the higher up on the body you place your focal point, the taller you appear. Take advantage of these ways to attract attention high on the body:

+ **Makeup** can focus attention on your face and make you appear taller. Even a small amount of makeup will do the trick. When tastefully applied, it's a great finishing touch that not only draws the eye upward, it makes you look more polished and put together.

+ **Jewelry**, such as a pair of earrings, a necklace or a brooch, uses sparkle, glitter or a small splash of color to attract attention close to your face.

+ **A hat** not only adds to your height, but when it has an upturned brim, it also draws attention up. Before you buy a hat, try it on in front of a full-length mirror to see how it looks with your figure and proportions. Never buy a hat with a brim that is wider than your shoulders.

+ **Details**, such as pockets, trim, buckles, and buttons, can create focal points. When strategically placed, they can attract attention anywhere on the body. To appear taller, keep the details on the lower part of your body more subtle. Details close to the face also draw attention away from the waist.

+ **Color** can create a focal point because the eye goes to contrast. Shiny fabrics, as well as light and bright colors reflect light and make the area appear bigger. To get the most out of this effect, try a contrasting wrap or scarf worn with a solid neutral color from the shoulders down. This splash of color draws attention close to the face.

Scale: Size Matters

Even when a garment fits your petite proportions, the scale of the print, the details of the garment or the exaggerated size of the accessories may not. To bring your wardrobe into sync with your physical appearance, you must make sure they match your overall scale.

Scale refers to the size of something in relation to something else. When two items of similar size are side-by-side, they appear balanced and in harmony with each other. If they differ too much in size, they appear unbalanced and out of sync.

Your body scale refers to your bone structure in relation to your height. Determining your body scale can be as easy as looking in the mirror. Does your bone structure appear small, medium or large in relation to your height? Analyze this proportion to determine your body scale.

The body scale of most women less than 5'4" is small to medium. As a shorter woman, you probably don't have a large bone structure. However, for a more accurate assessment of your scale, consider your features and apparent size as well. Do your features appear strong, delicate or somewhere in between? Is your weight average for your height? If you have very strong features, dramatic coloring and a fuller figure, your scale may appear larger than indicated by your bone structure and height alone.

Now that you know your overall scale, you can choose accessories, fabrics, and other details that complement your structure.

Keep Your Look Uncluttered

If you want to look taller, economize on styling details. Too many details—or details that are too large, too bulky or too bold—can overpower your smaller frame and make you appear shorter. Look for clothing with the following details in smaller proportions to complement your frame and height:

- Lapel widths
- Flaps, yokes and epaulettes
- Belts
- Buttons
- Pockets
- Sleeve widths

Select Appropriate Accessories

Accessories add the finishing touch that can tell the world who you are. Although fashions change and we each have our preferences, to look taller and more proportioned choose accessories that harmonize with your overall body scale and draw attention upward.

Small- to medium-sized accessories generally work well for petites, but that shouldn't prevent you from making a fashion statement. The key is moderation. Instead of wearing a large wrap, bold jewelry, chunky shoes, and carrying an over-sized handbag, select one larger or bolder accessory, or maybe two, and go easy on the rest. Think of your one bold piece as your signature accessory for the day. An uncluttered look with one signature accessory is always elegant and stylish. When choosing your signature accessory, remember that you are creating a focal point, so make sure it directs attention high on the body. Also consider:

+ The size of your handbag, as well as the length and thickness of the shoulder strap and any details on the bag.

+ The cut of your shoes. Sometimes a shoe fits the foot but the scale of the sole, heel and details are all wrong. If you like high heels because they add height, remember that if the heels are too high, they will appear out of proportion and make your legs look shorter.

Choose an Attractive Hairstyle

Hairstyles look best when they finish your look without overpowering it. For those of us with smaller stature, "big hair" is typically not the best choice. It can make you appear top heavy instead of chic.

When choosing your hairstyle, consider your frame, height and features. What do you want to accentuate? How can you appear balanced? For most women with a smaller stature, short-to-medium lengths work best.

Find Advantageous Fabrics

Choose fabric details that harmonize with your body scale. With a little strategic planning, you can use fabric to your advantage.

- **Prints and patterns.** Yes, you can wear prints and patterns. Just make sure to match them to your body scale. A low-contrast print with a dark background, or a non-descriptive pattern with no background, can fool the eye and camouflage the area. Prints also act as focal points. Keep the overall effect in mind for better balance.

- **Textures and weight.** Choose smooth or subtle textures and light-to-medium weight fabrics. They add less bulk to a smaller frame and make you appear slimmer than would thicker, heavy weight fabrics and rough, chunky textures. When you look slimmer, you also look taller.

Line: Create a Heightened Illusion

The cut, color and details of your clothing create visual lines. When used effectively, these lines can help you appear taller. The reason is because lines can fool the eye. Here's how lines work their magic: the eye automatically moves in the direction of the line and just keeps going—creating length or width, depending on the direction of the line. The longer and narrower the line, the more effective the illusion.

Choose Vertical Lines

Vertical lines help you look taller because the eye follows the direction of the line. A single line that runs from head to toe in the center of your body is the most effective. However, you can use any of the following vertical lines to your advantage:

- **Lines of Color.** Wearing the same color top and bottom creates an unbroken silhouette—a column of color. You can create a column with monochromatic tones as well, or by pairing light with light, light with medium, dark with dark, or medium with dark. When your stockings and shoes are the same tone as your hemline, the column becomes even longer, making you appear taller.

+ **Lines of Openings.** Layers also create lines. When you wear a closed jacket or blouse, a thin vertical line appears at the opening where the fabric overlaps. When you open your jacket to show a top that's the same color as your skirt or pants, you create a vertical column.

+ **Lines of Construction.** Vertical seams, single pleats, and slits on the front or back of skirts and dresses create vertical lines. Set-in sleeves make you appear taller than raglan or seamless sleeves.

+ **Creased Lines.** Lengthen your legs with creases ironed in the center of each pant leg.

+ **Lines of Closures.** Any vertically placed buttons, snaps, zippers or the like create a vertical line. The longer the row, the more effective the line. Single-breasted jackets create a taller look than double-breasted jackets.

+ **Stripes.** Striped fabrics and details instantly add vertical lines to your wardrobe. The narrower the stripe, and the closer it is to its neighbor, the taller you will appear.

+ **Standing Tall.** Posture and poise are non-verbal elements that instantly make or break your image. When you stand tall, your clothing hangs better, which enhances your body's vertical line. You not only look taller, you appear more confident, poised and powerful.

Minimizing Horizontal Lines

As with vertical lines, horizontal lines draw the eye in the direction of the line, so horizontal lines make an area appear wider. When something is wider, it automatically appears shorter.

Most horizontal lines are created by a contrast in color or texture, as in prints, design details, belts, or tops and bottoms in contrasting colors or tones. Although their power to make you look shorter may tempt you to avoid them altogether, a wardrobe with no horizontal details would be very boring. So to minimize their effect, use the following strategies:

+ **Space them unequally.** Wear horizontal lines in extremely unequal spaces to call attention to the upper part of the body. Keep horizontal lines on the lower part of the body subtle, with varied texture and finish rather than color.

+ **Balance them visually.** Make up for the effect of any horizontal lines on your bottom half by adding a focal point close to your face, such as a bright or contrasting scarf around your neck.

+ **Watch the accessories.** Any accessory that draws attention to itself horizontally will create a horizontal line. Either keep these horizontal lines high on the body or make them more subtle. For example, when you shorten the shoulder strap on your handbag, the horizontal line drawn by the bottom of the bag will be higher on your body. When you choose a handbag or belt in the same color or fabric as the outfit you're wearing, the horizontal lines they draw will be subtler than would be drawn by accessories in a contrasting color.

+ **Choose flattering shoes.** Elements of a shoe's design such as the toe, straps, and vamp (the area the foot slips into) can cause horizontal lines. To elongate the leg, choose a tapered or pointed toe rather than a wide, round or square toe; narrow, diagonal straps rather than ankle straps; and a lower vamp for a longer line.

+ **Evaluate your eyewear.** Depending on the style, the horizontal line your glasses create can be very strong or very subtle. The thicker the frame or the more contrasting the color, the more obvious the line. Although your glasses draw attention to your face, you want to make sure they also flatter your features, height and body scale. An easy way to defy gravity is to choose an upswept style that directs attention upward. Avoid eyewear with a downward sweep such as aviator styles. An extra touch of color on the upper frame or outer corner creates a focal point.

Keep your Hemline in Mind

Hemlines on skirts, pants, shorts, jackets, and tops automatically draw attention to themselves by creating a visual line of contrast. Follow these guidelines to minimize their horizontal effect:

- Keep your hemlines narrow by tapering skirts and pant legs in stiffer fabrics or by selecting drapey fabrics for A-line, flared shirts and wider pant legs. This shortens the horizontal line, which makes your silhouette appear narrower. The narrower your silhouette, the slimmer and taller you appear.

- Minimize contrast at the hemline by wearing hosiery and shoes or boots in the same color as your pants or skirt.

- Lengthen or shorten shorts and skirts to the most flattering part of the leg near or above the knee. This will keep the eye higher on the body.

- When wearing longer skirts or cropped pant styles such as Capri's, keep the line of the hem narrow and focus attention toward the face or coordinate a top or jacket in the same color to keep the vertical line long.

- Lengthen wider pant legs as much as possible to create a longer vertical line.

+ Although cuffs will shorten the leg, they also add interest. To compensate, tone your hosiery and shoes to the hemline or add a more dominant focal point near the face.

Let's Have a Fit!

Many retailers think that petite means size '0' or '2' with a shortened hem to accommodate our shorter legs. Many don't realize that along with shorter legs comes a shorter torso, shorter arms and narrower shoulders. This means that when you try on clothing made for the average-height woman, you'll likely find that the proportions are all wrong—the shoulders are too wide, the hem is too long and the waistline falls at the hips. Since most of the clothing sold in stores is made to fit a woman between 5'5" and 5'8," finding clothing that fits the petite women can be a challenge at the best of times.

In an ideal world, we petites would be able to walk into any store and find fashionable petite-sized alternatives. This is always your best option if you can find them. However, desperation may force you to purchase regular-sized clothing and try to make do. When browsing the racks in the standard-size departments, keep these tips in mind:

+ Choose clothing based on your body shape as well as your proportions.

+ Look at separates first; typically they are easier to fit than dresses.

+ Fitted styles will be harder to fit than eased styles. However, you'll probably be looking for tapered tops because they make you appear taller. This can present a challenge.

In the dressing room, you'll see that clothing that is too tight emphasizes your body shape in the wrong areas, while clothing that is too big adds bulk and makes you look frumpy. But your shopping trip doesn't have to end in frustration!

Alterations Can Save the Day

Purchase clothing that fits your widest areas and have the garment altered to fit properly. It will instantly make you appear taller. Your tailor can help you by:

+ Shortening hems and sleeve lengths
+ Taking in side seams on jackets, pants and skirts
+ Tapering sleeves, pant legs and skirts
+ Tapering or taking in side seams on tops
+ Taking in waistbands
+ Adding small shoulder pads
+ Removing cuffs on pants
+ Removing patch pockets on pants, skirts and jackets
+ Removing unflattering set-in sleeves on tops and dresses

Not Every Alteration is Worthwhile

While you're trying on those standard sizes, you need to know which problems are cost-effective to solve with alterations. Here are some guidelines to keep in mind:

+ If it doesn't fit in the shoulders and can't be remedied with small shoulder pads or taking in the back seam easily...
+ If the darts are in the wrong place...
+ If it's too long or too short in the rise or torso...

… Don't buy it unless the value of the garment outweighs the cost of the alteration.

Short and Chic for Life

Being short doesn't necessarily mean your personal dressing style must be boring, or that you can't stand out in a crowd like your taller friends. Fortunately, we can change how we appear with camouflage and illusion. The first step is to understand your own specific proportions. By understanding your body, you can use clothing and accessories to literally change what people see. The key is to find clothing or have it altered to work with the proportions of your body and its shape. Choose the right scale, lines, fabrics, and colors and you will appear evenly balanced, well proportioned and yes—taller.

KIMBERLY LAW, AICI CIP
Personal Impact International

Polish | Presence | Power

(604) 298-7228
kim@personalimpact.ca
www.personalimpact.ca

Kimberly believes that anyone can have a great image. With a little tweaking in one or more of the areas that represent a client's personal image, she can show them how to look and act their very best!

Kimberly is known for presenting her topics in an upbeat, non-threatening manner. She has been passionate about makeup and fashion ever since she was a little girl. Kimberly knows that looking great involves more than good clothes and makeup. Her desire to help women look their best prompted her to launch Personal Impact Image Management in 1999. As the founder of Personal Impact, she brings over 25 years experience in the area of personal appearance enhancement and personal marketing.

Personal Impact is a full service image consulting firm based in Vancouver, British Columbia, Canada specializing in all aspects related to personal appearance and etiquette. Kimberly was the first person in Western Canada to receive international recognition as a Certified Image Professional through the Association of Image Consultants International. She has been featured in the media across Canada as an image expert. She served on AICI's International Board of Directors as Vice President of Membership from 2004 to 2006.

Look Great During and After Weight Loss

Tips on Creating a Workable Transitional Wardrobe

By Kathy Pendleton, AICI FLC

Congratulations on your decision to improve your health through weight loss! In this chapter, I'll focus on the beauty and wardrobe needs of people who experience relatively rapid weight loss of 30 pounds or more. Why? Because people losing that much weight face special challenges not faced by people who lose less weight over a longer period of time.

Significant weight loss can affect more than your body shape and size. You might experience changes in the texture of your skin, hair, and nails. You'll progress through numerous clothing sizes, requiring many temporary wardrobe additions. When your weight stabilizes, you'll probably need to replace all of your clothes and adjust your body image to complement your new shape. By following the guidelines in this chapter, you'll maintain your appearance and keep your motivation high during your transformation, and you'll confidently create your new image when you've reached your goal.

It's important to take good care of yourself mentally and physically while you're losing weight. Create a list of things that you enjoy doing and reward yourself from the list as you progress. Take photos of your progress and keep a "wall of fame." Use accessories to give your wardrobe pizzazz, keep your spirits high, and project your personal style.

My own weight loss transition lasted five months. After losing the first 20 pounds, my wearable wardrobe was reduced to a few basic items: a long, black, elastic-waist skirt, jeans, sweatshirts, and a couple of oversized sweaters. I needed to go to work every day and present a professional image, but I was unwilling to invest in a new wardrobe every couple of months. I needed to figure out how to look great during the process while saving money to rebuild my image at the end of my hard-earned transformation.

Looking Great While Losing Weight

During my weight loss, I rejoiced in the changes to my body size and shape. Other changes were not so desirable: dry, brittle nails, lackluster skin, and thinning hair were unwelcome and unexpected. With care, however, you can address all of these challenges.

Maintain beautiful skin, hair, and nails. Your skin, hair and nails may become dry and dehydrated. Many weight loss diets drastically reduce the amount of dietary fats, including foods containing good fats. Some fats are necessary nutrients that cannot be manufactured by the body, such as omega-3 and omega-6 essential fatty acids. If you are concerned about dry or thinning hair, cracked fingernails, or dry, scaly skin, ask your health care or weight loss specialist about using an omega supplement.

If you haven't previously, begin taking great care of your skin. Maintaining elasticity as you lose weight could save you some surgery. Leaving your makeup on overnight ages your skin, so find a good, gentle cleanser and use it morning and night. Weight loss can contribute to wrinkles around the mouth and eyes, but many new products on the market can help. Moisturize, moisturize, moisturize!

Evaluate whether your skincare products are working well for you. Choose products that have a guarantee from the manufacturer or the store, so you can return them if you are dissatisfied. Be sure to test the product on a small patch of skin and leave it on for a few hours to make sure you do not have an allergic reaction to the product. If you do, take it back to the store.

Maintain a professional appearance during transition. It's challenging to maintain a stylish wardrobe while you're losing a lot of weight. A garment can usually be altered only one size, depending on the fabric and construction. The guidelines below will help you do several things: select clothes that camouflage the flaws in fit as your body shape changes, get the most wear from clothes you buy during your transition, and find economical places to shop.

- **Analyze your current wardrobe and clothing use.** Take a quick inventory of your current wardrobe. Note whether you wear mostly skirts or trousers. Is your clothing mostly for business or casual use? Can you dress more casually for work or comfortably dress up more during informal outings? Your answers will help you determine what you'll need while your size is changing regularly.

- **Set your budget.** I found that I dropped a number size every 10 to 15 pounds. If you lose about 10 to 12 pounds a month, that's a size every four to six weeks. If you're losing faster than that, you'll move through sizes and clothes

more quickly. How much are you willing to spend for a
skirt, jacket, or pair of trousers that you won't be able to
wear three months from now?

+ **Shop budget and secondhand stores.** The Junior
League and Cancer Society resale shops and the high-
end Goodwill Stores all have gently worn or even new
clothing, sometimes with the original tags still on. Look
for good-quality pieces that are basics and only one or two
seasons old. Stay away from distinctive trends from years
ago. Also, several major designers now have collections in
budget stores: Vera Wang is in Kohl's and Isaac Mizrahi®
is in Target. Outlet malls and second-tier stores such
as Off Fifth, a subsidiary of Saks Fifth Avenue, and
Nordstrom Rack, which is affiliated with Nordstrom, also
sell inexpensive, quality merchandise.

+ **Stick to dark, neutral colors and simple, classic designs.**
You can find clothing in these colors more easily, and you
can get by with fewer pieces. No one but you will notice if
you wear the same black skirt or trousers every day for a
week paired with different tops. Besides, monochromatic
dressing creates a long, lean line, and adding a pretty color
near your face draws the eye up.

+ **Choose skirts over trousers.** Skirts will last longer
than trousers in your transitional wardrobe. A friend of
mine who lost over 100 pounds found A-line skirts very
forgiving. She was able to nurse them along for a couple of
months by pinning the waist smaller and covering it with
a structured jacket. I preferred more flowing skirts with an
elastic waist, and I made sure that the waist was covered by
the top I wore.

+ **Choose sweaters for drape and jackets for structure.** A
basic structured jacket can work for you from the time you
can just fit into it until the structure is providing the shape as

you float inside. Don't buy loose, blousy jackets; your jacket should provide shoulder definition and waist shaping. You can buy a jacket that won't button closed if the gap is no wider than three inches; beyond that, it looks too small. Replace the jacket when it hangs off your shoulders. Often sweaters come in small, medium, and large and are designed to drape over the body. Choose those that drape beautifully, but don't look slouchy. Use that flow to your advantage while your body shrinks beneath it.

+ **Consider a neutral, versatile trench coat to extend your wardrobe.** It's a dramatic outerwear piece that you can wear indoors; it keeps you warm; it can cover a little extra fabric around your body as you lose more weight; and it can be belted to fit.

+ **Use a chart to help plan outfits.** Even if you don't have many garments, a chart can help you plan different outfits and get dressed quickly every day. It can also help in planning what might need to be replaced or what you might need to add to your clothing inventory. Below is an example of a wardrobe planning chart.

Bottom	Inner Top	Outer Top	Shoes	Accessories
Black skirt	Beige blouse	Short black blazer worn open	Black two-tone pumps	Long pearl necklace, pearl earrings, black handbag
Black skirt	Wine-colored camisole	Short black blazer worn closed	Wine-colored pumps	Long, narrow, print with wine color, rectangular scarf wrapped around neck, under jacket

• **Purchase special occasion clothing only if absolutely necessary.** Because these pieces are often expensive, avoid buying them during your weight loss. If you must buy a new garment, give yourself plenty of time to find what you need so you can stay within your budget. As one option, consider monochromatic separates in elegant fabrics, complemented by knockout accessories. On the other hand, this special occasion may be what started your quest to lose weight. If so, find something you love that shows off all your hard work and the changes you've accomplished.

+ **Take care of underwear.** Get fitted by an expert, and learn how she makes sure that the fit is appropriate, so you can help yourself. While your body is in transition, shop at the outlet malls to save money. You may be able to extend the wearing life of your bra by purchasing an extender to use with one band size smaller; as you shrink, remove the extender. You should have at least two bras. To extend the life of the elastic, never wear the same bra two days in a row and never put bras in the dryer.

+ **Use scarves and other accessories to add zip to your outfits.** These items you can invest in for the long term, so purchase classic, high-quality pieces that will last. A scarf can double as a belt to help cinch in a jacket and act as a blouse inside a snug jacket. Accessories can also direct attention away from a flaw and toward an area that deserves emphasis. Use a blouse, scarf, a lovely brooch, or earrings to draw the eye upwards to your face.

+ **Buy a full-length mirror.** It's impossible to evaluate your appearance without one. Elizabeth Hurley, the actress and beachwear designer says, "To look great, you have to be able to lethally assess your body and acknowledge the good and the bad bits." Buy a flat mirror without distortion, so you can evaluate your style regularly and accurately.

+ **Make wardrobe choices based on current body shape.** To determine your body shape or silhouette, stand in your underwear and put a light behind you so that your shadow is projected onto a wall or door. Your shape will be one of those listed below. Reevaluate your shape as you lose weight—because it's going to change! Aim to balance the top and bottom halves of your body by using clothing and color.

Shape	Description	Goals	What To Wear
Triangle	Your hips are wider than your shoulders	Emphasize upper body and waist to minimize lower body	Minimize lower half with dark colors, emphasize upper half with light or bright colors and structured jackets
Rectangle	Your shoulders and hips are the same with minimal waist definition	Define your waist	Wear straighter, drapey skirts, wear shaped jackets to create a narrower waist
Inverted Triangle	Your shoulders are wider than your hips	Emphasize lower body to balance wide shoulders	Wear darker colors on top to minimize shoulder width, avoid shoulder emphasis from jackets
Oval	Your waist and mid-section are wider than your hips and shoulders	Create or emphasize shoulder and hip shape to camouflage the middle	Wear well-tailored jackets with shoulder pads to create strong shoulder shape, wear drapey, straighter skirts
Hourglass	Your shoulders and hips are balanced and there is an obvious waist definition	The ideal woman's shape: Allow clothing to reveal your body's shape	Wear fuller, A-line skirts and jackets with pronounced shaping at the waist

For more details on body shapes, please see Elaine Stoltz's chapter, "Embrace Your Body Shape to Enhance Your Image."

Maintain your resolve and spirits. Keeping your spirits high helps to maintain your momentum and your commitment. When you look good, you feel good. Use these tips to keep your inner beauty shining through:

- **Build a photo history of your progress.** This can do wonders for your spirits. Take a photo every couple of weeks or so, depending on how rapid your progress is. Date the photos and display them where you can see them easily. This is your "wall of fame." It takes your focus away from the day-to-day process of weight loss and focuses your attention on the progress you've made toward your goal.

- **Reward milestones with your favorite activities or with hair, skin, or nail treatments.** A sumptuous facial, hair conditioning treatment, manicure or pedicure is a great reward for reaching a weight loss milestone. Decide on your milestones ahead of time, and then treat yourself with some well-deserved pampering.

- **Drink enough water.** Your skin needs to stay hydrated to look radiant, so be sure to drink enough water. Keeping well hydrated can also improve your energy and alertness. General dietary guidelines recommend eight 8-ounce glasses of liquid a day, which can vary based on exercise and other factors. Check with your doctor and nutritionist for the amount appropriate for you.

Keep it up—the rewards are worth it! This period of transition is an evolution, a time of many challenges and triumphs. You will learn about yourself: your resolution, weaknesses, values, and priorities. By following these tips, you will continue to look great and feel great! Grow, rejoice, and celebrate. Develop your sense of style before your reach your goal weight. Look through the style section at the bookstore or library and the other chapters of this book to help determine what your personal style will be. Take good care of yourself and do things that bring joy into your life.

Looking Great After You've Lost Weight

Congratulations! Now that you've reached your goal weight, it's truly time to celebrate. You're excited, energized, and eager to start building your new image. Your friends and family can see the new you, but often your own mental image hasn't caught up to the physical transformation. There are so many things that you're ready to take on now, it's difficult to know where to start.

I'd just like to interject a recommendation for restraint here. Since my weight loss four years ago, my weight has been more variable. I also found that I looked too thin at my goal weight and that I was unwilling to make the effort required to maintain that weight. For other participants in my weight management program, their weight loss slowed to a gradual rate, so they were unwilling to invest in a completely new wardrobe right away. Assess your own situation realistically and plan how you want to proceed.

Building your new image. Here are the steps:

+ **Assess the condition of the skin on your body.** Your skin will be looser after losing a large amount of weight. If you've lost over 100 pounds, you will probably have excess skin around your body. Consult a plastic surgeon to get an evaluation of how much you can expect it to adjust on its own, how much could be surgically removed, and how much treatment would cost. Surgery is expensive, and is covered by insurance only if it is deemed to be medically necessary.

+ **Get fitted for new undergarments.** It's important to wear foundation garments that fit properly. Your clothes will look better, and you'll feel better. Wait until you've achieved your goal weight or your weight has stabilized, because your breast size may change while losing the last few pounds.

+ **Use spandex and body shapers.** These foundation garments for the legs, derriere, and midriff can make a huge difference in the fit of your outerwear. See Bianca Stark-Falcone's chapter, "Foundation Pieces: The Secret Behind Every Beautiful Curve," for tips on how to use these undergarments effectively.

+ **Assess facial skincare and make-up.** Pay attention to skin texture and elasticity as you adjust your diet from weight loss to weight maintenance. For instance, if you re-introduce oils into your diet, you may find that the moisturizer you're using is too heavy. The shape of your face may have changed dramatically, too. Consequently, your make-up products and practices may need to change to fit your new look. Be flexible now and over the next six months as your skin continues to adjust to your new size and your maintenance diet.

+ **Consult a good hair stylist.** If your face is narrower now, you may need a different style to achieve a pleasing balance. Seek the help of a good hair stylist who can recommend styles to suit your new face and personal style. You may want to leap into a new style, or you may want to take it slow.

+ **Allow your shape to show.** You've worked hard to achieve this new body shape, so now is the time to show it off. I don't suggest wearing skin-tight clothing, but be open to trying fashions that skim your new figure. Clothes that bind and squeeze are going to add pounds to your look anyway.

+ **Hire an image consultant.** A professional will see the new you, without the bias of having known the "old" you. Once she's helped you to define your new style, you'll be ready to go shopping. Have your image consultant take you shopping, or contact a personal shopper at your favorite department store. Tell her that you're interested in wardrobe basics, have just lost a lot of weight, and will eventually replace your entire wardrobe, but currently you want to spend only, say, $400 or less. When I did this, my personal shopper brought me mostly sale items, but also wardrobe basics of excellent quality (although not on sale). I appreciated her approach, because it meant that she understood my wardrobe plan.

+ **Go for it**. In working with a stylist, promise yourself that you'll try on everything. Some things will work and some won't, but you'll never know if you don't try them on. Give yourself plenty of time to experiment with different looks, because 90 percent of what she brings into the dressing room should stay there. So, try it on! The benefits will show in your wardrobe as your new style develops.

+ **Start with the basics**. You already know how to get by on a minimum number of garments, so start by replacing these basics with high-quality items that fit perfectly. See Rosa Maria Livesay's chapter, "Creating a Winning Wardrobe."

Revel in Your Success. Let me end by offering a thought from Frederic Fekkai, hair designer extraordinaire: "Most women are not aware of their beauty—they're most aware of their defects."

Be aware of your own new beauty. You've succeeded in changing your physical shape. You're moving on to changing how you use that new shape and style to project your own physical and inner beauty into the world. By using the strategies outlined in this chapter, you'll find that building a new style to show off the new you is a manageable and enjoyable process.

KATHY PENDLETON, AICI FLC
Style Developer

Life's too short to blend in!

(650) 279-0980
www.curveycouture.com
Kathy@curveycouture.com

After losing fifty pounds over a five-month period, Kathy was inspired to pursue her interests in fashion, personal style, and skincare. She began her career in image consulting by selling a line of carefree, reasonably priced women's clothing called CAbi, and loves the versatility of the line.

Kathy studied extensively with style guru, Alyce Parsons, and became a certified Universal Style Consultant. She joined the Association of Image Consultants International and served as secretary of the San Francisco Bay Area Chapter for two years.

Based in the San Francisco Bay Area, Kathy is passionate about helping other women achieve the image they desire as they go through their weight loss transitions. Her specialties include consultations in fashion, skin care and image changes associated with dramatic weight loss.

Camouflage for the Curvaceous!

Work What You Have With Confidence

By Sonya Barnes, AICI FLC

Not all of us are built like actress Gwyneth Paltrow or fit into a size 2 or 4. It amazes me that manufacturers continue to cut many of the top quality garments for pencil-thin models. They can't possibly live in the real world. Real women have curves in a variety of places. They may or may not be wearing plus sizes. However, the clothes I see that are straight, with no room for my curves, I deem as not "woman-friendly." Not woman-friendly means those clothes were not made for me, a curvy woman with hips and serious thighs. As an image consultant who works with women who aren't typical Hollywood glamour types, I find it my duty to "seek and teach" them how to accentuate and honor our curves without being dismayed or looking like Vienna Sausages squeezed into ready-to-wear (RTW) clothing.

I want to address three of the most common figure challenges with simple techniques on how to camouflage without drawing attention to the more voluptuous parts of the body. First, I will address each figure challenge, provide a solution and finally, suggest my professional garment recommendation.

There are some "Curvy Rules of Order" to keep in mind. The mantra is Fit, Comfort and Ease. Always ask yourself:

+ Is this the best fit?
+ Is this comfortable?
+ Can I move easily while wearing this?

Curvy Woman Figure Challenge #1:
Small Waist and Full Hips

The number one question I hear from "women with curves" is "where can I find jeans and pants to fit my derriere without gaping in the waist? We will answer that million-dollar question not just for jeans but also for slacks in general. Every manufacturer cuts their garment differently; meaning the waist-to-hip difference will vary according to the fit model. Sometimes this can be as small as seven inches or as big as ten inches. Simply stated: all sizes are not created equal! A size 8 in Dana Buchman® may be a size 4 in Ellie Tahari®; which for me is not a "woman-friendly" brand.

Solution: Ladies, as hard as it may be to do—forget the number! We give it way too much power. I worked with a client who swore to me she was a size 6 and had been all her life. Looking at her body measurements and armed with my knowledge, I knew better. "I've always been a size 6, I don't know what happened," she said after selecting a pant that fit her bottom without pain, in a size 10. I told her to let it go and "own the number." The easiest solution for this is to fit the largest part of your behind and have the waist altered to fit you accordingly. Now that's not rocket science, but ready to wear is NOT ready to wear for most.

I would say that some manufacturers are more generous than others, so I'll let you in on a few industry secrets.

Let's start with the infamous "what jeans can fit my derriere?" I've found that denim can be the most deceitful piece of clothing a shopper can encounter. Being knowledgeable about the manufacturer is one thing, but when they make five or six different cuts of the brand it really gets confusing! We read magazines and see the latest jeans on the latest glam girl and off we go to the store only to find they don't quite fit like the magazine promised. Frustration arises. Look for a maximum of 2 percent Lycra, as this is just enough to give a bit more room after a few wears, but not so much that they fall off of you in a month's time. The denim jeans I've chosen are not trendy, low-rise "suicide for your behind," but hit at the natural waist with a modern cut. Update your denim! It's the new black pant! For a more personalized fit, I recommend visiting www.zafu.com. This site provides you with a personalized questionnaire and jeans that fit specific requests.

Denim Jean Favorites for Curvy Women

+ David Kahn®, found at Nordstrom® and specialty boutiques
+ AG Jeans, the Club®, made famous by Oprah
+ Joe's Jeans®, the Honey®
+ Citizens for All Humanity, the Amber or the Hutton®
+ Seven for All Mankind; the Jenny boot cut®

Recommended Slacks for the Professional Curvy Woman

+ Dana Buchman, my tried and true. I recently found out she will be doing a line for Kohl's® department store so many flagship stores such as Nordstrom and Macy's® will eventually fade her out. However, she is a great choice for the curvier woman.

+ Ellen Tracy® is a classic favorite. She gives you room for the present and future possibility of any weight fluctuation.

+ Jones New York®

+ Lafayette 148®

+ Classique® from Nordstrom

+ Ann Taylor's Margo® and Lindsay® pants have been consistent for me over the past three years.

Curvy Woman Figure Challenge #2: Large Thighs

Women who have a full bottom also typically have larger thighs to match!

Solution: Fuller thighs require that the pant have a fuller cut through the thigh. The guidelines I use for full bottom I apply to full thighs for obvious reasons. Another option would be to choose an A-line skirt or dress that falls over the bottom half.

Proper Jacket Length. Jackets frame the upper part of the body, so construction and hemline are critical components in camouflage technique. Jackets that stop above the hip or exactly at the hip create a horizontal line that adds width to the widest part of your hips. Jackets that come below the waist and skim over the hips create the illusion of oneness. Jackets and bottom pieces of the same or similar color work best.

Placement of Color. If you can remember two things, remember these: light expands, dark recedes. Wherever you place the darkest color, attention will diminish, or be taken away from, that particular area. That being said, light on top and dark on bottom will naturally draw the eye to the lighter part. The light area will appear larger. So placing lighter on the bottom will draw attention to that body part. So does this mean we can't wear white pants or a white suit? Absolutely not! If you wear a lighter bottom, the key is to bring the eye away from that by adding a striking print to your top. Wearing an eye-catching piece of jewelry or more intense make-up on eyes or lips will keep attention above the shoulders during communication.

Texture and Pattern Placement. Now remember, just because they make it, doesn't mean it's for you. I swear by these words. One thing to remember about texture is that it, too, adds visual interest. So wherever you add texture, prints, and patterns, attention will be drawn to that area. This means if you wear pants or skirts that have a pattern—particularly pants—you are saying, "look at my bottom." Palm trees, monkeys and other "cutesy" patterns in bright colors on pants or Capri's create a conversation below the waist.

Curvy Woman Figure Challenge #3: Full Bust

If this is your figure challenge and you're bursting at the seams, then consider these simple solutions outside of surgery.

Solution: Hold them up! First and foremost, invest in a great bra. And I do mean a great bra! Oprah Winfrey has put the stamp of awareness on women wearing the wrong size bra. Remember what I said earlier about owning the number? Same rule applies here. This is critical, not only for comfort, but for support. It's amazing the visual effect that a great bra does for "the girls." If, of course, it is causing you health issues, please seek additional medical advice. Remember to go for fit, comfort, and ease.

Fabric Selection. When choosing a top for a full bust, the more ease, movement and drape the fabric has, the more flattering. Look for fabrics that create a draping effect, preferably in dark colors. Matte jersey, draping silk, and quality knitwear provide you with room for ease. Some of my favorites are: Donna Karan, The Collection®, St. John Knits®, and Misook®. If your choice for a top or blouse is cotton, look for a cotton-Lycra blend so no imprints show. Now I can hear some of you saying, "What about the classic white button-down shirt?" Well, here's the key: it's a wardrobe staple, but the tricky part is the opening of the button holes. I had a client who loved the classic shirt. Every time I saw her, there was gaping—and many times you could see her bra and skin beneath! I finally advised her that if she was so headstrong to continue to wear the button-downs, instead of going up a size, which caused fullness below, how about we look for button holes that opened horizontally versus vertically? Who would have thought? This allows for the natural spread of fullness, not fighting against a vertical line. Now that was worth her weight in gold. She of course has "stretched" herself by her awareness of fabric construction talk, not to mention comfort.

Prints, Patterns, and Other Details. Remember what I said about full hips? Wherever you put a lighter color or colorful, bright print, this is where the eye will travel. Now, before you blast me out of the water saying I advised a full-busted woman not to wear prints, consider this: Choosing prints of appropriate scale, meaning large or small, can give the illusion of oneness. It's like a kaleidoscope. You see all the colors at once; your eye doesn't stop at each color. Prints whose scale fit your body structure and don't look like refrigerator magnets stuck on you will work great.

If you love stripes, know that stripes create a horizontal line, possibly adding weight and making your bust look wider and fuller than it actually is. My personal opinion is to approach with caution. Minimizing details on a full chest is another thing to think about. Patch pockets, bows or buttons placed on a top garment draw attention to that area. It still amazes me to see 44DD's donned with pink bows or red flowers at their bust. Keep it simple.

Business Jackets. Even with current business casual practices, a suit or at minimum, a jacket is required for work. When purchasing a jacket, a full-busted woman should consider the number of buttons on the jacket. My first recommendation is the three-button jacket. It creates a vertical style line, elongating this area and helping to minimize gaping, which is often seen with a single button and sometimes a two-button jacket. Now, consider where the jacket opening begins. A lower jacket opening, just above the fullest part of the bosom is more flattering than the turtle in the shell look.

Some of my favorite manufacturers for a curvier woman with full-grown "girls" are:

- Donna Karan, The Collection
- St. John Knits
- Misook
- Chico's®
- Eileen Fisher®

Now you're armed and dangerous just enough to say, "Whew!" Let's quickly review key concepts when addressing your curves:

First, don't apologize for them! People are paying good money to get what we were naturally given. Since when did bottoms become so popular? The actress and singer Jennifer Lopez is not the first with a bodacious bottom. I'm older and had it first! Seriously, when we view our curves as a true positive and carefully camouflage what we don't want to let the world in on, it's magical.

Remember the "Curvy Rules of Order": fit, comfort and ease.

Placement of patterns and color, and minimizing extra conversation pieces, will distract the eye from that area. And remember, just because they make it doesn't mean it's for you! My grandmother used to tell me, "Everything ain't for every BODY!" Work with what you have with confidence!

SONYA BARNES, AICI FLC
Harris & Barnes Image Consulting

Excellence by choice

(704) 540-0989
sonya@harris-barnes.com
www.harris-barnes.com

Sonya Barnes, President of *Harris & Barnes Image Consulting*, a professional development company, is a certified image consultant and an associate member of the AICI. She has received formal training by the world's leading image masters in color, style and wardrobe development. Possessing strong leadership skills, she is known as the "go-to" consultant for many of her peers, and often sought out to speak to many private and public organizations and provide workshops and seminars on visual appearance, and verbal and non-verbal communications.

She is a founding member of the Atlanta AICI Chapter where she has served on executive committees including VP of Communications, VP of Programs and Chapter President. In 2008, she earned an appointed position on the International Board of AICI as VP of Education, overseeing the education and ethical aspects of the trade association.

She is a faculty member at the internationally renowned London Image Institute based in Atlanta, Georgia where she serves as Master Trainer for style development and menswear, as well as corporate image and communications. Sonya's company has now expanded globally to include clients in Singapore and Hong Kong where she teaches the business of image and brand strategy.

Above-Average Style For Full-Figured Women

Creating A Wardrobe That Lets You Sleep In Monday Mornings

By Heather Elrick, AICI CIP

All women should have access to current fashion and style. However, recent statistics show that the average woman stands about 5'4" in height and weighs approximately 163 pounds. It is also common knowledge that at least 43 percent of North American women are larger than average, and are not being served adequately in stylish boutiques. We're talking about almost every other woman. This above "average-sized" woman lives life exactly like her smaller-sized counterpart. She's involved in either a corporate or domestic career—or maybe even both—and she probably plays golf or swims, falls in love and gets married. She's a vital, active and successful woman and the fashion industry refers to her as being "plus-sized."

When it comes to outfitting our closets, stylish plus-size selections are often hard to find. However, manufacturers and designers are beginning to respond to the beauty needs of "real women." It's taken some time, but we can now finally create a wardrobe that any full-figured woman can be proud of! Younger styles come in vibrant colors! We can get well-proportioned fits, with no more frills or flowers! Comfort without the frump and soft, exotic fabrics that drape and sizzle. It's time to be loud and proud about who you really are and dress the part of a modern woman.

Nothing Succeeds Like the Appearance of Success

The first step in projecting ourselves as competent plus-size women begins with understanding the role played by personal imaging and what it has to say about us. The expression that "you never get a second chance to make a first impression" is well known, but do we live by those words?

There are eight factors that immediately register within the first few seconds of meeting someone. Five of these we have control over and three, we don't. Initially and subconsciously, people note your gender, race and apparent age. There's no denying or changing any of that. The last five factors that typically form a lasting impression include:

+ **Your clothing.** Does it fit properly, is it clean and pressed, coordinated and an appropriate look for the environment and occasion?

+ **Personal grooming.** Is your hair styled, makeup appropriate, breath fresh and your deodorant applied?

+ **Facial expression**. Sincere, friendly and smiling or tired from the night before?

+ **Body language**. Welcoming, interested and open; or arms crossed, anxious and "closed off?"

+ **Eye contact**. Direct—indicating sincerity—or darting everywhere but where they should be?

Which of these points has the greatest impact? Interesting enough, it's the clothing and grooming and not your stellar, verbal introduction. And, as an above average-sized individual, it's the category that relates to personal appearance that also poses the greatest challenge for us.

Developing your personal image is anything but a light-hearted matter. In today's society, personal appearance is responsible for up to 55 percent of any first impression. We are perceived as being successful if we look competent and capable. If our dress is sloppy, outmoded or mousey, we will be judged in that light. From the job interview to the PTA meeting, or even at a neighborhood barbecue, how we look and how we dress will be one of the most important messages we convey about ourselves. Don't worry, here are some great ideas to ensure that you easily send the message you want in every life situation.

You're Late! You're Late! For a Very Important Date!

We've all had them, right? It's known as the "bulging closet but nothing to wear" type of morning and the scene typically opens with you standing in front of the closet, flipping through hanger after hanger. Nothing matches, it's going to be a fat, bloated day; the laundry didn't get done, nor the dry cleaning picked up and you definitely don't feel like wearing that green blouse!

When most of our closets are already bulging at the seams, how come that 'right look' just never seems to be there for us when we really, really need it? We've invested in all of our favorite matching pieces in all of the trendiest colors and still we stand and stare. The solution? You inevitably grab "whatever."

The answer to your Monday morning "what to wear" dilemma is found within a mini collection of pieces hanging in the middle of our closet with a sign overhead reading "Professional Attire." To the right side of this grouping sits another collection for our weekend wear, and on the other side you might find glitzier pieces for special occasions. This little grouping of professional attire is simply a collection of five to twelve individual pieces that mix and match perfectly with one another. Once you've done your homework, this mini grouping will initially create ten different looks and as you add to it, more combinations will become available.

First Things First

When it comes time to making a decision on whether or not to include a specific garment in your core grouping, it must be hands down, exactly what you need and have been looking for. For example that classic white shirt that you just tried on, is it the best shade of white for your skin tone? Does it pull across the back, even just a little, or does the button gape inappropriately you know where? All these minor details will come into play Monday morning when you're rushing around and *really* need a blouse to wear. If wearing this particular garment doesn't make you feel like a million bucks and put a smile on your face every time you wear it, take a pass and keep looking. You'll be glad you did.

Secondly, as women, we're famous for making excuses. And, as plus-size women, it may be even more difficult for us to find that perfect fitting, right colored garment. Remember our goal? Every piece we want to add to our grouping must mix and match perfectly with its counterparts in order to create the maximum number of looks possible.

And last but not at all least, we really must touch on why that jacket and pant just doesn't seem to flatter you as well as you'd hoped; or even why certain garments look better on someone else despite the fact that you both wear the same size! It all boils down to one thing: your silhouette and the role it plays when getting dressed.

Silhouettes

The word "silhouette" actually has two different meanings. First of all, it can refer to the generic shape of your body. At the same time, it can also refer to the shape of a garment, and the shape the garment will create once it is on your body. For example, the silhouette of a full-cut skirt will enhance an already rounded bottom half and make it look even more curvaceous than it already is. A tailored, straight-cut, pencil skirt would be a more flattering choice. If you have a prominent tummy that curves into a full hip, reach for the straight cut skirt with an elasticized waistband and you'll find it works even better.

Body silhouette descriptions (such as pear, rectangle, oval, hourglass and inverted triangle) relate to everyone, regardless of size. So, on one hand someone can have an hourglass body shape and wear a size 4. On the other hand, someone else can have another hourglass shape and she'll wear a size 24! That's all it is. You can refer to Elaine Stoltz's chapter, "Embrace Your Body Shape to Enhance Your Image," to learn how to identify and work with your own unique silhouette.

A successful shopper needs to marry the silhouettes of body shape and garment design in such a way as to create the most flattering look possible. Yes, it does take time and patience to find the most perfect pieces you could ever imagine. Take a moment and think back to the last time you received a compliment. Do you remember how big your smile was and how tall you stood? Now imagine feeling like that all the time. That's our goal.

When out shopping, choose styles appropriate for your body shape. It's important you understand the basics of how this process works and why it succeeds! If you know what styles of garments to look for, you'll find your jaunts to the mall more efficient and less time consuming.

A Foundation to Build On

Start with a basic jacket, skirt and pant. If you need to purchase any of these pieces, always invest in the best you can afford. The payoff will be a well-made garment that you'll grow tired of well before it's time to replace it.

This core grouping should be in no more than two neutral colors that can be worn together (i.e. black and grey, navy and red; brown and cream). If possible choose a mid-weight fabric. This is where the investment part comes in, because now you'll be able to wear these pieces pretty much all year round. You'll be able to update your look with these same pieces seasonally and year-to-year with lesser-priced garments, trendy colors and accessories. Add panache and flair to your "winter suit" in the spring with lighter, seasonal accent colors. For example, try a navy cardigan with an apple green tank or a brown jacket with a petal pink camisole. Accessorizing with scarves or jewelry showcasing both colors will help pull the look together and create a winning combination without needing to spend a great deal more.

Your pieces must fit and flatter your body shape as it is today, not after you lose those next ten pounds. Clothes that are too tight will focus attention on problem areas, whereas clothes that are too big will actually make you appear larger. Honestly. Your best look will be found with tailored garments that allow ease of movement and comfort. That also means having your hems and sleeves altered so you don't look as if you borrowed an outfit from your big sister's closet.

I cannot overstress the importance of good foundation garments and shape wear. Nothing dampens a stylish look quicker than inappropriate bulges from VPLs (visible panty lines) and a sagging bosom. If the idea of magically losing another ten pounds appeals to you, I suggest you invest in a professionally-fitted bra; one that will lift your breasts up to where they should be, which is roughly half way between your shoulders and waistline. Having them sit up where they were meant to go will instantly open and lengthen your torso, as opposed to having your tummy and waist appear to blend and become part of your bosom. Enough said.

Visit your specialty boutique for fittings and tips and yes, lingerie stores for full-figured women are starting to appear! If there's not one in your neighborhood, get fitted at Nordstrom or Macy's, and then check out the local Wal-Mart or Target where they now host a vast array of bold colors and patterns in the latest, luscious feminine wear. For more information, see Bianca Stark-Falcone's chapter, "Foundation Pieces: The Secret Behind Every Beautiful Curve."

When it comes time to add to your wardrobe, follow the same principles of quality, fit, and color with future additions of coats, novelty jackets, vests, sweaters, dresses, and Capri pants or walking shorts.

Additionally, you will discover:

- Better quality pieces will provide **value** for the dollars spent.

- You will develop a sense of **consistency** with your personal image as opposed to the "hit and miss" approach to getting dressed, producing a magnificent boost to your self-esteem and **confidence!**

- You'll appreciate the **versatility** of being able to take a blazer from one part of your closet and combining it with a tee and pair of well-loved jeans, creating a casual, yet chic look for weekend wear.

- Building a wardrobe will **save time** and yes, enable you to sleep in.

- You will save money and **rescue your budget!**

Mix-and-Match Magic!

With the following eight pieces, you will be able to create a minimum of ten looks, if not more:

- **Slim, knee-length black skirt**. The simpler in design the easier it will be to dress it up with a cardigan or longer, tunic blouse or go casual, with a jean jacket. An a-line or straight cut skirt will probably best suit a shapely bottom, rather than enhancing the roundness with a fuller cut silhouette.

- **Two-piece cardigan sweater set**. Worn together or as separates, the versatility alone makes this investment worthwhile. There are so many style options today that we can no longer wave off the idea, consider it matronly and belonging only in Mom's closet. Yes, as shapely women we can wear knits. I consider Oprah, Camryn Manheim and Queen Latifah as high profile role models, and they most definitely show off their well-rounded shapes! With foundation garments that allow the knit to glide and slide across the body, you'll find the look capable of enhancing curves wherever intended.

+ **A two-piece jacketed suit**. Not necessarily matching, but rather any two pieces that go together and create a chic, tailored look. This may include a jacket with a dress pant or skirt, or for a more casual lifestyle it could even be a vest and matching slacks.

+ **Casual trouser**. Anything other than denim and capable of looking great either with your jacket or sweater set. A straight or moderate boot cut to the pant leg suits most plus-sized body shapes, and will balance out the fuller hip. A tapered pant will only emphasize a rounded upper body.

+ **Classic white shirt**. Ensure buttons don't pull across the chest and that it appears crisp and bright-colored all the time! Continuous laundering will eventually dull a bright white so it may be wise to invest in a couple of these, given that they're a wardrobe staple. Look for spandex content; it means that it will be comfortable to wear, move with you and help the garment to hold its shape. Spandex garments will last longer if you hang to dry rather than using a hot dryer.

+ **Basic tees and tanks**. I consider these pieces accessories, and suggest you not invest in expensive labels, thereby allowing you to freely change colors and styles. If you do find them on sale, buy multiples!

Plus-size specialty boutiques may be a wee bit difficult to discover. However, these retail chains are good starting points: Chico's (to a size 18), Lane Bryant and The Avenue. Macy's has a women's department while Nordstrom has the Encore department. There's also Catherine's and The Fashion Bug. Get

247

creative and search the Internet, where you'll find these and many more destinations that you can either visit personally or shop with online.

Pulling It All Together

The secret to combining these pieces into multiple combinations is to view them all as individual garments. A suit is traditionally meant to be worn together as one look and a sweater set is after all, a set. However, when the pieces of suits and sets are considered as separates, new combinations will appear. Try hanging these pieces in your closet in a non-traditional manner. Instead of hanging your suit jacket beside its matching bottom(s), consider hanging your jackets, cardigans, and vests together; your bottoms—meaning skirts, dress pants and casual trousers—next; and finally tops such as blouses, sweaters, and tee shirts. Organizing your closet in this manner will showcase these garments in a new light and allow you to visualize new combinations. Here are a few outfit suggestions to get you started:

+ Your basic black skirt, cardigan from the sweater set and a white shirt

+ Jacket, casual trouser and tee

+ Sweater set with black skirt or with your dress pant, or with the casual pant. That's three outfits right there!

+ Jacket with its matching dress pant and classic white shirt. Switch out the shirt for the camisole for a dinner date!

That's already seven looks and I haven't even gotten started! The rest is up to you and one last little tip: all of the above looks are based on working with three pieces. With a two-piece look, like a simple top and bottom, you will have even more combinations available.

Color: The Secret To Success

Choose a complementary color palette to work with, beginning with two, and no more than three colors; for example, navy, grey, and pale blue. Remember that black and the various shades of white and cream will go with most colors of a basic wardrobe, and that more than likely you already have appropriate pieces somewhere in that bulging closet of yours!

You will find greater success with mixing and matching if you start with all solid colors. I suggest reserving prints and mixed textures for your accessories and lesser-priced pieces, such as sweaters and scarves, to add interest.

One suggestion is to wear a navy jacket and grey bottom with a printed tee featuring navy, grey, and pale blue. You've worked within the established color palette, created a coordinated look and not blown the budget because you found a less expensive piece that flattered your two investment pieces. Next time around, try the same jacket and pant with your white shirt and accessorize with pearls and a chunky bracelet—a classic look that no one would ever question!

Your goal is to assemble a core wardrobe, with fabric, colors, and silhouette successfully woven together. Once you've achieved this milestone, you will have the satisfaction of knowing that each and every time you get dressed you will be capable of presenting the strong, memorable first impression you've always dreamed of.

Add-on Accessories

Avoid the ordinary! Small accessories on a larger-sized woman appear insignificant and only point out how much bigger she really is in comparison to whatever is being worn or carried! Webster's Dictionary describes proportional comparisons as the "correct size between one thing and another." For example, tiny pearl drop earrings, small petite prints or even tiny evening bags will all appear out of proportion with a plus-sized woman. Consider instead a big chunky bracelet or a magnificent signature pin for your jacket lapel. Hollywood has made the over-sized clutch popular; it could be the perfect accessory for your next special occasion.

Check your full-length mirror and see whether the shoes you've chosen truly complement your outfit. Some flats have a tendency to make us appear grounded, whereas wearing moderate heels can create a slimming effect. You can also simply shorten the hem of a skirt and wear flats, ballerina slippers or sandals, easily creating a look more pleasing to the eye.

Accessories magically transform any outfit and there are at least twenty-five pieces you can use to change the looks of your core wardrobe. So rather than becoming bored with a few quality pieces, check out these lesser-priced investments: totes, umbrellas, and handbags; low-slung belts that lengthen the torso and slim the upper body; hats and boots. Look for chunky bracelets for casual wear, classic jewelry for the office, and don't forget pins, scarves, detachable collars for jackets and coats, or even changing out your jacket buttons. You can also change hairstyles, makeup, fragrance and nail color to create an entirely different look with the same core wardrobe pieces.

You're Big. You're Beautiful and Yes, You Are Unique!

Today, there are media campaigns currently being shown that are more forward thinking. To their credit, these campaigns are promoting a new industry standard that embrace any and all as unique and beautiful! Photo shoots feature women of all sizes and shapes, young and old. Each and every one of them is simply beautiful. You see it in the eyes here and the smile there. The strong curves and soft, petite silhouettes are not shy but upfront and bold! They're actually glowing, standing their ground while daring you to think otherwise. Bravo! Well done. Now, imagine all of us having that same courage to say out loud and accept what these ads so eloquently share!

As image consultants, one of the most basic services we provide is showing women how to develop their own, unique personal image. We're delighted that recent advertising campaigns have had enough courage to "break all the rules" and express what we've always believed: that the "above-average" sized woman can have style too.

As you move forward in building your image keep in mind personal style is a feeling we have about ourselves; it is self-confidence expressed visually through our choice of fashion. Don't compromise ever again. If you don't feel like a million bucks, keep looking. You'll be glad you did! A strong and memorable impression is yours when the finished look fits and flatters your luscious plus-size figure. If the pieces you've lined up in your closet are easy to mix and match, you will be able to sleep in on Monday mornings!

HEATHER ELRICK, AICI CIP
Panache Plus Personal Styling

Mastering Fashion Quandaries For The Curvaceous Gal

(604) 931-4595
helrick@shaw.ca
www.panacheplus.ca

Internationally-certified image professional Heather Elrick believes that *all* women should have access to current fashion and beauty needs. As a result she specializes in dressing the curvy, above-average woman stylishly and with flair! A lively, energetic and entertaining public speaker, Heather gives fun, fact-filled presentations and workshops that empower participants with the knowledge that they too can look just as fabulous as their petite counterparts. Heather provides this unique fashion resource through her firm, Panache Plus Personal Styling. Industry and media accolades continue to support Heather's "passion for plus-fashion."

An avid fashion magazine junkie, volunteer cosmetician and "Beijo Bag Lady," Heather is a member of the Association of Image Consultants International, the professional affiliation for image consultants worldwide. In 2004 Heather earned recognition as a Certified Image Professional (CIP), one of the top advanced certifications available to consultants in the fashion industry.

Fifty is the New Forty

Looking Fabulous at Any Age

By Judith Ann Graham, AICI CIP

I met Clarissa just before her fiftieth birthday. Her husband bought her a makeover session with me because as he put it, "she deserved it." He described his wife as a terrific mother of three, a loving wife (she was his high school sweetheart), and a world traveler. Having lived in Europe, Clarissa developed a keen eye for fashion and learned how to sew for her petite frame. Because she was a trained artist, she mixed together colors, patterns and fabrics with the ease of a brush stroke. For Clarissa, fashion was just another expression of art. She was cultured, educated, with an above average style IQ, and enjoyed expressing her creative side. Yet, in the couple of years leading up to her husband's phone call, she began to refer to herself as a "schlumpadinka," an Oprah "ism," referring to one who wears baggy sweats and T's. Clarissa felt the need for a change, but was completely stuck in a time trap. Her smartly tailored skirts and jackets had been replaced with a closet full of jeans for all occasions. Her hair and makeup regimen consisted of home hair coloring, with an occasional cut, and her makeup was non-existent. No longer living in Europe, Clarissa moved to suburban America where her lifestyle was casual, erring on careless. In short, Clarissa's appearance slowly sank into a fashion depression with little hope of recovery.

The past fifteen years had changed her emotionally, physically, and hormonally. She felt younger than she looked, though she doubted she could look ten years younger, plus she had no idea where to start or what to do. Clarissa needed much more than a fashion police party; she needed a trauma team intervention.

Can a woman over fifty drink from the fountain of youth and still look age appropriate? This chapter will focus on how you can erase ten years from your looks without undergoing invasive surgery or expensive extremes. I will share the secrets of younger-looking skin; beautiful, sexy hair; and age-defying body tips. This is why my clients come to me. Looking fabulous over fifty is my gift to you.

Part 1: Facing the Facts

The media screams in our face—young, younger, youngest! Yet, a Merrill Lynch study found that "seventy-six percent of the boomer generation intends to continue working well into their 'retirement' years." The pressure is for women to look younger, smoother, fresher and firmer. But, the facts of aging are just the opposite. Our skin begins to sag, wrinkle and get duller as we age. By the time we reach fifty, the tracks of time have visibly altered our faces from fabulous to "fabu-less." The urge to start addressing the signs of aging begins as we see crows' feet creeping around the eyes. Then, it's panic time and a race to find the perfect "hope in a jar." In our forties, our skin loses elasticity and we begin seeing worry lines in the forehead, frown lines between the eyes, puffy, dark circles around the eyes, and then laugh lines around the mouth. By the time we turn fifty, we see saggy jowls and double chins. Thank you, age demon!

What causes skin to sag and age? The answer is our metabolic and circulatory systems begin deteriorating. As the years go by, the nutrients that feed these important systems are compromised. The result is normal cellular breakdown. Nothing can stop this process but science and technology are continuously offering us a diverse menu of skin enhancing treatments. A few women—I'm not a member of this club—covet their wrinkles as well-worn tokens of time and tears, claiming to have earned them in life's war zones. However, most of us battle wrinkles as much as we battle the newfound bulges we never had before.

Where Wrinkles Come From

What causes wrinkles? Every skin professional agrees that sun exposure is the number one culprit leading to skin damage. Stress is the runner-up to sun exposure, but since neither the sun nor stress can be entirely eliminated, having wrinkle-less skin well into our fifties and sixties becomes a challenge. The medical journal, *Plastic and Reconstructive Surgery*, states that surgeons are "experiencing increased competition from dermatologists and skin specialists, particularly concerning facial procedures," according to the New York Times article, "Dr. A-List Can See You Now," by Natasha Singer. Lasers, injectable fillers, muscle relaxers, cellulite reduction, and skin rejuvenation have become refined, advanced and affordable to the degree that women now have effective options. In short, the number of women scheduling plastic surgery is decreasing due to superior non-invasive procedures.

If you are wondering which non-invasive procedures are right for you, go shopping for a qualified, cosmetic medical doctor's office. Be sure the doctor is available to consult with you, can explain what is best for your skin and is well versed in up-to-the-minute treatments. A dermatologist may not be your best source for beautiful skin enhancement, so shop around. However, first you must know your skin type and how to care for your skin.

Cleanse, Exfoliate, Moisturize

Cleansing, exfoliating, and moisturizing are the ABCs of beautiful skin. Skin specialists agree the worst mistake a woman makes is neglecting her skin. All the trips to your skincare salon are a waste of time if you don't take care of your skin daily. If you don't know what type of skin you have—oily, dry, combination—and don't know which products are best for you, take the time to have your skin evaluated by a professional. Get in the habit of using high-grade cosmeceutical products that treat and protect your skin.

Cosmeceuticals are products containing pharmaceutical or prescription strength ingredients that deliver appearance-enhancing benefits. If your skincare budget allows for only one high-grade product, target a particularly troublesome area. After all, you have only one face and it is exposed to the climate every day, so SPF protection is a must. As we age, hormonal changes cause the skin to become drier and more sensitive, with less elasticity. Factually, our skin is the largest organ of our body, yet we don't treat it like our other organs. We spend hundreds on designer labels but often we are a bit stingy with our skin. I also recommend a good quality automated facial brush, such as Clarisonic®. It cleans the skin more thoroughly and allows skincare treatments to penetrate the skin deeper. Saving your face is worth the effort!

Let's Talk Skin Technology

Lasers. Lasers, or light technology, have become routine in nearly every medical office and spa. Lasers are constantly improving and penetrating deeper into the skin's dermis layer. They are used to correct fine lines and wrinkles, smooth the texture of the skin, reduce acne, and help tighten and re-sculpt the face. As we hit fifty, tightening, smoothing wrinkles, and firming skin is our objective. Lasers work with light pulses that target a specific area and stimulate our natural collagen production. The result is a firming effect of the skin that is otherwise loose and lax. Fine wrinkles are reduced, lifting is noticeably present and the skin's texture appears smoother. If you are striving for more lifted, smoother skin, have a discussion with your skincare professional about the latest advances in laser technology.

Fillers vs. Relaxers. Allow me to clear up the difference between fillers and relaxers. Fillers are injected into the skin to plump up lines, creases and folds. Muscle relaxing injections such as Botox® relax the muscle group that causes lines resulting in limited movement, or causing a temporary "muscle freeze." Both fillers and relaxing products must be injected into the targeted areas of skin but the results are completely different.

Filler Injections. Fillers injected into the skin replace our own collagen that has broken down and become depleted. Fillers are used anywhere on the face where we want a natural, smoother look—with movement, but less noticeable creases, lines and wrinkles. Fillers soften these areas, but do not "freeze" them so we have total mobility. Fillers are effectively used on frown lines between the brows to avoid an "angry look" and work well in the laugh lines around the mouth and cheek areas. One advertisement that promotes filler injections shows a woman smiling with the caption "parentheses have a place but not on your face." Fillers will plump-up unwanted facial lines with immediate results and long-lasting benefits.

Botox. Botox is most effective when you want a particular muscle group to have less mobility: the forehead is a perfect example. When Botox is injected into the forehead, what is achieved is a smoother forehead with little ability to contract those muscles. The result is a higher eyebrow arch that gives the illusion of lifted eyes. Of course, many of us have seen a trigger-happy Botox user who looks like a frozen Mickey Mouse. But generally, Botox refreshes the face. The results can be seen within a day and can last up to six months depending on the individual. Once it is absorbed into the body, the forehead will return to its original lines and mobility. Groucho Marx would not have wanted Botox injections, as he would have lost his trademark ability to raise his eyebrows. Botox is not for all areas of the face; for example it is not for use around the lips where you want—and need—mobility. At one time Botox was feared to be a toxic substance that was released into the body, but it is time-tested and safe.

Lip Enhancement. As we age, our lips become thinner and less even. The upper lip is the first to go, then the lower lip. Lip sculpting is a crucial and delicate balance to the face. Unfortunately, too many women end up with "trout mouth" from overly enhanced lips. The desired result should be proportionately fuller lips that are smoothly contoured and compliment the face. If lip enhancement is one of your main concerns, be sure to consult a trained expert. Before you get a lip enhancement treatment, consider filling in the smile lines first. Lip sculpting is performed using an injectable gel-based filler that lasts many months with immediate results.

Cellulite Reduction. In an ideal "Stepford Wife" society, cellulite does not exist, but for 95 percent of women it is part of the normal aging process and part of normal body anatomy. Even though it is normal, most of us consider it unsightly and unattractive. The good news is that there are marvelous advances in cellulite reduction that are virtually pain-free and needle-free. Dissolving unwanted cellulite requires a commitment to a series of treatments and regular maintenance due to the fact that the fat cells will not stay away unless they are "tricked" into staying away. With advanced technology, cellulite reduction can be performed with virtually no side effects. The result is even, smooth skin with no lumps or bumps commonly experienced in less advanced treatments.

Peels, Masks, and Facials. The medical breakthroughs mentioned above are more effective in treating wrinkles, lines and sagging skin, but there are other treatments that clean, resurface, and restore moisture to the skin from an aesthetic point of view. These are the treatments you get from a non-medical spa or salon. Peels are designed to remove dead skin cells and encourage collagen production. Peels can also assist in lightening sunspots, age spots and even out the skin tone. Masks are marvelous treatments used for a variety of results. There are hydrating masks, soothing masks, calming masks, invigorating masks, and so on. Your skincare specialist will recommend a mask appropriate for your skin's condition. Facials, as well, serve many purposes, but the main purpose of a facial is to clean the skin, thoroughly removing blackheads, whiteheads, and other build-up on the skin's surface.

Skin Sense. With advancing technology, we will have more choices to consider and with it, more confusion. Beautiful skin does not come without a price, but taking care of our skin only requires a commitment. As we change, our skincare must change with us. Use richer products during the fall and winter and less heavy products during the spring and summer, all containing SPF. Choose your skincare specialists carefully and wisely. Free trial treatments could cost you dearly, ruining your skin due to inexperienced or untrained personnel. We've heard the horror stories; don't become the next victim. Be gentle, but firm with your body's largest organ. Your skin is nature's velvet coat.

Part 2: Now Hair This

Nothing changes a woman's appearance more than a new hairstyle. And here's the good news: as we age, our hair actually improves in texture and manageability. So let's celebrate this fact and consider what to do now. Wearing hair too light and too short is the biggest mistake women make. If you can't remember the last time you changed your hairstyle, it's time to talk with your hairdresser.

Hair Color. Many of us face graying issues as we age and want to cover the gray or lighten the color. Oddly enough, the hair ages fastest of all, so that by the time we reach fifty we don't remember our natural hair color. Colin Lively, former head colorist for the Elizabeth Arden Salon, recommends looking at pictures from your childhood and taking your color cues from your youth. "Your hair color should be in the same tone in your fifties as it was before you were a teen." If you were a redhead, you should be a softer version of red today. The same is true for brunettes: a softer, subtler version suits you now. And one more tip: if you never were blonde, don't become one. If you are graying and love it, work with it so the hair has shine and sparkle. That means a trip to the hair colorist to blend in your gray.

Avoid ashy or brassy tones, as both are aging and unflattering and leave the hair "flat" looking. Your hair color should never be more than two shades darker or lighter than your natural color. If you are home-coloring your hair, try to apply it like a professional: first the roots then a few minutes on the ends. Applying hair color throughout the hair results in a mess that looks worse with each application. That's how the hair becomes too blond, too pink, or looks like shoe polish. Treat yourself to a professional colorist and adjust your color to something soft, pretty, and age-appropriate.

Hair Cuts and Styles. The texture of our hair changes dramatically as we age. Curly hair becomes less curly and our hair gets thinner. The average head has three million hairs but the circumference of each hair gets thinner with age. Most of us think we are losing our hair, when actually it is getting thinner. Some women experience severe hair loss that can be devastating. Consult a hair loss professional to consider natural, permanent hair options. Hair also becomes duller, lacks luster and gets drier with age. This brings up the issue of long hair. Some women refuse to give up their long locks thinking it makes them look younger. Honestly, a head of long hair on a fifty-something face is likely to add ten years. If you are one who wears your hair constantly in a clip or ponytail, it's time to cut your hair. The mistake is that too many women wear long hair in styles that look best on younger women.

So what is the best length? Short is fine but it must be cut to complement your face. Broader faces need more volume, whereas narrow faces need the hair sculpted around the face. Our generation has been told that women over forty should not have long hair. Not true; it's a matter of how one wears long hair. Having your hair layered and angled around your face is terrific. Throw in some hot curlers and give it some body and volume. Voila! Now you have gorgeous, sexy, long hair. Long hair requires effort, so give it the attention it deserves.

One of the best styles to consider is the bob. The definition of a bob is hair worn from chin-length to shoulder length. Classic

Chanel bobs are shorter in the back, longer in the front. Bobs can be worn layered or blunt cut. The versatility of a bob looks great on nearly every face shape and is easy to manage. Good stylish cuts that suit us withstand the test of time. Notice women such as Nancy Reagan, Jane Fonda or Barbara Walters. Their basic styles have not changed for decades, but they constantly make subtle changes as they age. Consult your hairdresser for a haircut and style review. Ask if your style is serving you now and should you update it. Many of us have long-standing relationships with our hairdressers and we end up talking about the cat rather than our cut. If you think you need a new, fresh opinion, start shopping for a salon.

Part 3: Breasts, Bottoms, and Body

Breasts. In general, we go through life not liking certain parts of our body, but as we age, for some of us, we have more parts we don't like. Yes, body sculpting, breast enhancement, etc. are available, but most of us learn to accept our bodies and deal with aging. There are, however, certain guidelines we need to know about as we move into our fifties. As menopause kicks in and gravity descends upon us, we enter unfamiliar territory of bodily changes. What once worked with diet and exercise no longer does the trick. We have to change our eating habits, step-up our exercise routines and work harder to simply stay the same weight. Our metabolism slows and many of us experience slower energy. Even if we do maintain our "younger" weight, our body shifts: adding a thicker waistline, lower bust line and broader behinds—and that's just for starters. What are we to do?

From an image point of view, there are several "fix it" solutions that will help turn back the clock. As we age, our breasts and bottoms drop a half-inch with each passing decade; thank you, gravity! Smaller-busted women don't notice the shift as much as a larger busted woman. But the reality is that most women never change bra sizes and furthermore, don't know their correct bra size. One of the biggest mistakes women make is wearing the same bra they wore when they were younger, one that does not address the gravity issue. As one bra fit expert once said, "You can't let those old dogs hang down, you need perky puppies." Rather than advise on bra brands, it's best to make an appointment with an expert and find out your true size and best fitting bra. Even if you are an A-cup, look for bras that lift, separate, and have adequate support. Allowing our breasts to hang down drags down our figure. Furthermore, an ill-fitting bra adds extra weight to our mid-region, and we can do without that! See Bianca Stark-Falcone's chapter, "Foundation Pieces: The Secret Behind Every Beautiful Curve."

Bottoms Up. There are no buts about it: our behinds get broader with age. They also sag and collect cellulite. Most of us realize our rears need extra coverage, though few of us know how to address it. Like a supportive bra, the same is needed for our derriere. These days, we have loads of options for a firmer looking bottom. Look for high tech fabrics that are lightweight but have plenty of control to firm and smooth. The English refer to a cherry picker truck as a "lift and shift." This is a fairly accurate description of what women should be looking for in an undergarment designed for our bottom half. There are undergarments designed to lift and smooth the entire mid-section as well as the bottom. Most importantly, find your correct size and don't try to squeeze into a size smaller or you will end up passing out from the struggle to get into it. Panties, hosiery, one-piece garments, even slips, have firm support and control. You will need a variety to wear under different outfits. You will want one version for casual wear, another for suits and business wear and still others for evening wear. When your undergarments are worn out—generally about a year's time with normal wear—throw them out. The whole idea is to have a slimming, streamlined, uplifted silhouette. Women can have lovely skin and a great hairstyle, but give away their age because they don't invest in proper undergarments. It may sound harsh, but the English are right: we need a "lift and shift!"

Body. As we age, many women hate their arms, refusing to wear sleeveless garments. As an image expert, I recommend to cover up what you don't like, show off what you like, and for the rest of the body—thank God for industrial strength spandex! We cannot wear the same fashions we wore in our twenties, nor can we compete with our much younger daughters. Perhaps you have great looking legs and want to wear shorts. Put on a pair and study yourself in a mirror. Do your knees look rippled? Do you see spider veins? Do your ankles appear thick? If so, re-think wearing shorts. Skin specialists report that, "If you are wondering how old a woman is, look at her hands." Short of intense treatments, you can use hand lotions with retinol or glycolic ingredients to smooth away dead skin and lighten age spots. Remember to wear gloves for protection from cleaning products and harsh weather. When showering or bathing, use products that exfoliate and hydrate the skin. Also, reduce the amount of time spent bathing, as long showers and baths tend to cause extra dry skin. We must realize that age goes hand-in-hand with drier skin. We feel it in our lips, our eyes—and do I need to add—other body parts, too? Yes, there are rejuvenation treatments for that, too.

Remember, you can control a lot of the aging process and can slow it down. Yes, a lot of it has to do with genetics, so develop a beauty regime that includes regular facials, stress-reducing exercises, and professional hair care treatments. Seeking the help of dermatologists and plastic surgeons can also help to stave off the look of aging. Most importantly, think young and don't forget to moisturize, moisturize, moisturize and you will absolutely look ten years younger.

JUDITH ANN GRAHAM, LLC

Your guide to a revolutionary new you

212-688-3202
800-NYC-LOOK (692-5665)
jag@judithanngraham.com
www.judithanngraham.com

Judith Ann Graham, a former Miss New York State in the Miss America organization, is a personal wardrobe stylist and hair and makeup expert focusing on women over 40. A native Virginian, Judith began her career in New York as a model and actress. She won several roles in television commercials and daytime dramas including *All My Children*.

As a style expert she is a frequent guest on TV networks such as CBS, FOX, ABC, NBC, and the show *Late Night with David Letterman*. Though her makeover services empower clients to look spectacular at any age, Judith is also a corporate speaker on dress-for-success topics. She is a certified member of the Association of Image Consultants International, Fashion Group International and teaches at the Fashion Institute of Technology. Judith Ann Graham helps her clients discover their personal style with ease and elegance.

More Image Power

Now that you have all you need to know to truly build your image power the next step is to take action. Get started on your own by applying what you have learned in the pages of this book.

When you are ready for one-on-one image consulting from any of the co-authors in this book—we are available! We provide a variety of services and you can find out more about each of use by reading our bios at the end of our chapters or by visiting our websites. For your convenience, each co-author is listed below by geographic area.

California

Cheri Bertelsen, AICI CIP, CDI   www.cbcolorandimage.com
Helena Chenn, AICI CIP   www.helenachenn.com
Marjory DeRoeck, MFA, AICI CIP   www.theimagestudio.biz
Marion Gellatly, AICI CIM   www.powerful-presence.com
Rosa Maria Livesay, AICI FLC   www.rmlimages.com
Kathy Pendleton, AICI FLC   www.curveycouture.com
Bianca Stark-Falcone, AICI FLC   www.bwelldressed.com

Colorado

Dana Lynch, AICI FLC   www.elementsofimage.com
Leah Oman, AICI CIP   www.thesmarterimage.com

Georgia
Sarah Hathorn, AICI CIP   www.illustraimageconsulting.com

New York
Judith Ann Graham, AICI CIP   www.judithanngraham.com
Catherine Schuller, AICI CIP   www.divabetic.org

North Carolina
Sonya Barnes, AICI FLC   www.harris-barnes.com

Oregon
Bernie Burson, AICI FLC CDI   www.bernieburson.com

Texas
Elaine Stoltz, AICI CIM   www.stoltzimage.com

Washington
Deborah King   www.finaltouchschool.com
Molly Klipp   www.aloetteofseattle.com

CANADA

Ontario
Wendy Buchanan, AICI, LO   www.perceptioneyewear.com

Vancouver
Heather Elrick, AICI CIP   www.panacheplus.ca
Kimberly Law, AICI CIP   www.personalimpact.ca